FANNING THE FLAMES OF INTERCESSION

By Mike Bachelder

DAN & AMY
MAY Your own
Journey be blessed.
Mike

Copyright © 2016 by Mike Bachelder.
Printed by BT Johnson Publishing
www.BTJohnsonPublishing.com
1-866-260-9563

Unless otherwise noted, "Scripture taken from the New King James Version.
Copyright © 1982 by Thomas Nelson, Inc. Used by permission. All rights
reserved."

"Scripture quotations taken from the Amplified® Bible,
Copyright © 2015 by The Lockman Foundation
Used by permission." (www.Lockman.org)

Scriptures marked as "(GNT)" are taken from the Good News Translation -
Second Edition © 1992 by American Bible Society. Used by permission.

Scripture quotations are taken from the Holy Bible, New Living Translation,
copyright ©1996, 2004, 2007, 2013, 2015 by Tyndale House Foundation.
Used by permission of Tyndale House Publishers, Inc., Carol Stream, Illinois
60188. All rights reserved.

American Standard Version, King James Version, The Message – Public
Domain

Printed in the United States
All Rights Reserved.

ISBN: 978-1-938311-28-4

DEDICATION

I would like to dedicate this book to my wonderful wife Darla, who has walked with me every step of the way on this journey to discovering the heart of God through intercession. Her gracious willingness to, in the early days, stay home with the kids while I went on intercession journeys to many places around the world. And in the later days, travel with me to many places, as well as live overseas in Scotland for nearly 3 years, missing tremendously our kids and grandkids. She has sacrificed greatly and I could not do most of what is described in this book without her. Together with her, we are always poised and "quite ready for another adventure."

ACKNOWLEDGEMENTS

I am grateful to:

My kids, Erin, Kristi, Amy, Michael and Jessica, for their patience, understanding and willingness to let me travel the world (sometime with them along) in this journey. Of course, I am also grateful to them for our wonderful grandkids.

All the pastors, leaders, family and friends who have poured into my life over the years.

The "Watchmen"; Jeremy, Emily, Marilyn and Liz. Amazing intercessors and true friends. What we had in the Lord for those few years was truly special.

Finally, my spiritual father and mentor in intercession, the late Dr. Frank Hultgren. He was such a guiding light during the early years of my journey. He was a great man and dear friend.

INTRODUCTION

Prayer, intercessory prayer and intercession... Words used to describe one of the most powerful and dynamic privileges of the Christian life. It is one of those topics most Christians would say they have at least a bit of knowledge about. To most people though, it is a spiritual truth that they have barely scratched the surface of. It is actually one of the best kept secrets through which God fully releases His life-changing, miracle-working and divine-enabling power to bring change into the world we live in. I pray you will be encouraged, enlightened and inspired as I have endeavored to bring together solid biblical truth with exciting stories of my 21-year journey to discover the heart of God through intercession.

This book isn't designed to be an exhaustive teaching on intercession and spiritual warfare. Then on the other hand, it's not to be just a group of random stories. What I want to share are the lessons I have learned in my journey to become a person of prayer. My prayer for you is that the story of my journey will be a blessing to you and help you step into this wonderful, powerful and amazing privilege called intercession. Your own journey awaits you... just let Him fan the flames

~Mike Bachelder

TABLE OF CONTENTS

Chapter 1

THE IMPORTANCE OF INTERCESSION

I n this chapter we will be building a case for the absolute importance of intercession by believers today. To understand the importance of intercession, we must first come into clarity about the dynamics of true intercession. Once we have understanding as a foundation, then we can move out in confidence and be effective in this vital ministry.

Intercession Defined

Let's define intercession. I have found that if I can discover the root meanings of the words involved, it will help me come into greater understanding of that topic. Let's look at the root meanings of the word "intercede," which is the basis for the words intercession and intercessor. The Strong's concordance definition of the word in the Hebrew is *"paga"* which means *"meet together with the connotation of creating a meeting."* The idea is that our intercession releases God to encounter man and bring change to situations in this present age we live in. The Strong's concordance definition of the word in Greek is *"entugchano"* which means *"to chance upon, confer with, to make ready or bring to pass."* The thought here is to passionately get ahold of God in prayer to make ready and bring to pass His desires in a situation.

The dictionary definition of the word intercede is this, *"to move or pass between, to mediate, intervene on behalf of another, to act between parties with a view to reconcile those who differ or contend."* The idea here is of a courtroom setting with one party representing another. This is exactly what is going on as we stand before God's throne, the heavenly courtroom, and represent others with our intercession.

Here are some quotes from a few authors that might be helpful as we get a grasp on intercession and what it is really all about:

Norman Grubb from "Rees Howells Intercessor"

"Perhaps believers in general have regarded intercession as just some form of rather intensified prayer. It is, so long as there is great emphasis on the word 'intensified'; for there are three things to be seen in an intercessor which are not necessarily found in ordinary prayer: identification, agony and authority." The word "intensified" means *"travail, importunity, weeping, groaning"*. (Strong's)

Dutch Sheets from "Intercessory Prayer"

"Mediation defines intercession and intercession defines mediation. As can be seen clearly in these definitions, the concept of intercession can be summarized: mediating, going between, pleading for another, representing one party to another, but not limited to, legal situations."

Beni Johnson from "The Happy Intercessor"

"My definition for being an intercessor is 'capturing the heartbeat of heaven and declaring or praying that into my world.' It's true agreement with heaven."

Here is a definition that I have come up with to try to make it as simple and straight forward as possible.

"Intercession is God giving an individual a piece of His heart (an intercessory burden) to passionately pray back to Him, thus releasing the power of the Holy Spirit, the ministry of angels and the activation of the church to perform His will and establish His kingdom. In its simplest form, it is FOCUSED PRAYER FOR OTHERS."

Standing in the Gap

In defining Intercession, we will need to look at what it means to **"stand in the gap"** in prayer.

We find a great picture of intercession in Ezekiel 22:30, *"And I sought for a man among them that should make up the **hedge**, and stand in the **gap** before me for the land, that I should not destroy it: but I found none."* The Hebrew word for **hedge is "gader"** which means *"an enclosure, wall or fence."* The Hebrew word for **gap** is **"perets"** means *"a break, a breach, breaking forth.* The idea is that there is a gap in the wall and that we need to stand in that gap to prevent the enemy from breaking in.

Also the **gap** in the **hedge** is the picture of a battle line, and the need to fill any gaps in the line. Ezekiel 13:4-5 illustrates this well, *"O Israel, your prophets are like the foxes in the deserts. You have not gone up **into the gaps**, neither **made up the hedge** for the house of Israel to **stand in the battle** in the day of the LORD."*

2 Corinthians 5:18 speaks about the **gap between God and man,**

and how intercession is a vital part of the "ministry of reconciliation" that we have received from the Lord. Another analogy we can draw from the concept of "the gap" is the **break in a power line** that would stop the flow of power. Our intercession will be instrumental to reconnect the flow of the Holy Spirit into a situation and release His power to bring about change.

Intercession - Why and Why Not

Why We <u>Shouldn't</u> Have Intercession.

Before we get into the reasons why we should have intercession, let's look at some of the reasons why some have said it should be avoided. Over the years I have heard many good rationales from some pastors, leaders, and others about why we **should not** have intercession. Here are some of the reasons they gave:

1. Too Risky and Hard to Control

They have heard scary stories of, or experienced firsthand, when things got out of control. When it comes to things we don't understand, what we often do is react. Often what we feel uncomfortable about is what we perceive to be an extreme. We shouldn't **REACT TO AN EXTREME BUT RESPOND TO THE TRUTH.**

Bill Johnson said, "Reaction to error creates error." There are two extremes of intercession, especially in meetings. One extreme is an anything goes, heavy on the manifestations type of approach. Reacting to such an extreme, in an attempt to be safe, often means going to the other side which is no intercession at all. The problem is, no intercession equals no power. We need to respond to the truth. An illustration of what it's like when we cut off the power supply that comes through intercession is like having a car but refusing to put fuel in it, or having an electric tool and trying to use it with no battery pack.

Because many have seen some extremes in intercession, they have a tendency to have a "throw the baby out with the bathwater" reaction, instead of trusting God and the truth of scripture. I remember once I was in a pastors meeting with a group of area pastors. All of a sudden I felt the leading of the Holy Spirit to say something to the group. I said, "As pastors of churches there are times in our prayer meetings when a spirit of intercession is going to come into the meeting and people will begin to weep, cry and travail before the Lord. You know, guys, when that happens we need to just let it happen." I looked at the pastor who sat next to me and he was white as a sheet. He said, "Uh, what if I just did that (shut it down) … last night." I said. "Well brother, I believe that you now have a word from the Lord not to do that."

When it comes to strange things happening in meetings, many have quoted the verse that says, *"Let all things be done decently and in order."* (1Corintians 14:40). The question we need to ask is, "What is heaven's definition of descent and in order?" If you look at the scene around the throne in the book of Revelation, there are elders throwing down crowns, eye balls everywhere, thunder and lightning and all kinds of activity. This is heaven's definition of decent and in order. Once again, I'm not condoning strange activity for the sake of strange activity. But we need to be open to the Spirit of God coming into our meetings and releasing the spirit of intercession.

Now I am all for leadership and there are definitely times to bring adjustment to a meeting, but let's make sure our leadership is by the Holy Spirit and not by a fear of things getting out of control.

Intercession is one of the elements that will enable us to bear fruit in our lives and ministries. Jesus is expecting fruit but we must remain connected to the vine. Intercession is one of the ways we connect and remain connected. If, because of fear, we disconnect from Jesus, we will have a difficult time bearing lasting, quality fruit (John 15).

1. Intercessors are Weird People

Often intercessors are seen as the nuts, flakes and fruits of the church. I can say this because I am an intercessor. To the natural or religious mind, the outward expressiveness of many intercessors is perceived as unusual, weird and maybe demonic.

A number of years ago in North Carolina I had the privilege of painting the house of an international prophet named Bob Jones. As a group of friends and I were working on the house, there were a few of Bob's personal intercessors there as well. Bob was not home at the time and they were marching around the outside of the house doing all kinds of prophetic acts. They did everything from waving banners to anointing the house with oil. One of the guys working with me on the house commented, "Man those intercessors are weird." I chuckled and said, "Yeah,

I'm one of those." He quickly replied, "Oh I didn't mean you." I just laughed. What my friend didn't realize was that what seems foolish in the natural mind can actually accomplish very much, first in the spiritual realm and then by releasing blessing into the natural realm. As intercessors we are often called to do strange things, but we should strive to be as normal as possible in our everyday lives.

As one who has led intercession groups for years, I have seen my share of strange intercessors. Some of them are still in a process of healing and restoration and have fallen into the snare of trying to gain approval or acceptance by attracting attention to themselves. As people of prayer, we need to always invite the Holy Spirit to check our motives. But when it comes to us judging another person on their outward expressiveness, we must be careful. I remember visiting a new church that had one of their intercessors right up front during worship. Without thinking I said to myself, "Oh great, there is another one of those 'flaky' intercessors." The Holy Spirit abruptly chimed in on my thought. "Excuse me, but can I talk to you about this woman? You have no idea what she goes through every week, so don't judge her for her outward expression of worship and her love for Me." I quickly repented to the Lord. I came to find out that this very woman was married to an atheist. She would go home from church every week and be persecuted for her faith. In the midst of that persecution she was a powerful woman of prayer.

Once again let's not throw out intercession just because of the outward expression of intercessors. I think, as the body of Christ, we need to do more to honor the intercessors that God has given us.

2. Intercession is Just for Intercessors

Many have the idea that intercession is only for a small, select group of spiritual intercessors in the church or ministry. I firmly believe that God lays His hand on certain individuals to go before the throne and make intercession as a primary focus of their particular ministry. The only problem is that some have the idea that, because this group is functioning, they are not needed to intercede. This makes about as much sense as saying, "It is good that we have worship leaders so we don't have to worship," or "I'm really glad we have evangelists so I don't have to share my faith with anyone." The argument that intercession is just for "intercessors" just doesn't hold water. Paul says, "*I exhort therefore, that, first of all, supplications, prayers, **intercessions**, and giving of thanks, be made for all men; for kings, and for all that are in authority; that we may lead a quiet and peaceable life in all godliness and honesty. For this is good and acceptable in the sight of God our Savior*" (1Timothy 2:1-3). In these verses I can see no indication that Paul is speaking only to intercessors.

In Luke 18:1 we read, "*Then He spoke a parable to them **that men** (not just intercessors) always ought to pray and not lose heart.*" Every believer is to take part in the priestly ministry of intercession which is referred to as the "Royal Priesthood." (1 Peter 2:9; Revelation 5:10).

I believe there is a level of intercession in which every believer can function. It may be as simple as praying for your family, friends and church, but even in that we are all called to intercede.

There are some who are called as intercessors and then there are those, the rest of the body of Christ, who are just called to intercede. Let me illustrate. In 1998 I went with a group of intercessors to Fez, Morocco to do onsite intercession for the country. Fez is the religious capital of Morocco, as well as the place where the founder of the country is buried. God had given us a specific strategy as to how to pray, which He had confirmed to us prophetically, so we were ready to go.

As we were waiting in Gibraltar to board a ferry to take us to Tangier, Morocco, one of the sisters on the team told me she was quite confused. When I asked her what was wrong she told me that she really didn't know why God would want her to be on this trip." As I questioned what she meant, she said "Well I am not an intercessor, so I don't know why God would send me on a trip with a group of intercessors." To which I replied, "Well can you pray?" She responded, "Yes I can pray." Then I explained to her that God wants her on this trip, because God wants all of us to pray. As it turned, out God used her to pray some powerful prayers for the people of Morocco on that trip. No one had any doubt that she was supposed to be there.

In this day, I think God's plan is to get as many people praying as possible. Let's encourage the brethren everywhere to pray.

3. Does it Really Make a Difference?

Many believe that intercession is optional because they don't believe it really accomplishes anything. Some might say, "After all, haven't we done just fine so far without it?" What they are really saying, especially in the western world, is that we can do church, religion and what looks like kingdom work quite well without God's power, presence and anointing. Many of us seem quite content to do the same thing, year in and year out, and get the same result. I think it is high time for this mindset to change.

I remember having coffee with a brother that I was meeting for the first time. When he asked me about our ministry, I said that our main focus was intercession and intercession training. I was quite surprised at his response when he said, "Oh yeah, intercession. I was part of a denomination and we used to talk about intercession 20 years ago." I thought to myself, "You used to **talk about** intercession 20 years ago?" I wondered what he had been doing for the last 20 years without the foundation of intercession in his life and ministry.

The Bible and church history are full of stories of God giving specific answers to the desperate prayers of His people. Does intercession make a difference? **ABSOLUTELY!**

Why We <u>Should</u> Have Intercession

We have looked at some of the reasons for not having intercession, now let's look at the reasons that intercession is so overwhelmingly important.

Every time I share this teaching, whether it is in our school of intercession or just around a table with some friends, I am that much more convinced of how tremendously important intercession is as one of the primary callings of the body of Christ today. Let's look at some of the reasons intercession is so vital.

1. God Chooses to Work Through the Prayers of His People

2 Chronicles 7:14 says, *"IF My people who are called by My name will humble themselves, and pray and seek My face, and turn from their wicked ways, then I will hear from heaven, and will forgive their sin and heal their land."* By starting this verse with **IF,** God is indicating that He plans to cooperate with the prayers of His people to see things accomplished. This means that if we do not pray, there is that which will not be accomplished. Try to imagine God poised as if standing at the starting line of a race. He is there with tremendous desire to move in the lives of people and show Himself strong on their behalf. Usually a race begins with a certain sound. The sound that God is waiting for is the sound of our intercession reaching heaven. Just like in Daniel's prayer, his voice was heard in heaven and the angel was dispatched (Daniel 10:12). It is very important that we do our part and pray.

As we cooperate with God, we are also in the school of the Holy Spirit to learn what it means to rule and reign with Him. One of the books that inspired me in my early days in the 1970's was by a man called Paul Billheimer. He said in his book, "Destined for the Throne", that prayer was "on the job training." This is what he said, *"The explanation is that prayer is not primarily God's way of getting things done. It is God's way of giving the church 'on the job training' in overcoming the forces hostile to God. God designed the program of prayer as an 'apprenticeship' for eternal sovereignty with Christ. The prayer closet is the arena which produces the overcomer."*

Like Oswald Chambers said, *"Prayer does not fit us for the greater work, prayer IS the greater work."*

2. It Brings Heaven to Earth

In Matthew 6:10 we read, *"Your kingdom come. Your will be done on earth as it is in heaven"*. We want to see all the goodness of heaven released on earth. We want to see God release from heaven real answers to real problems in real situations in the lives of real people. In a sense, our intercession reaches in to heaven and pulls down divine power saturated with the DNA of heaven.

One of the benefits of intercession is that it keeps us rooted in the eternal realm. As we stay in close intimacy with God, we find that heaven begins to have more sway in our lives than this natural realm. As we are praying for others, we cannot help but connect to the heart of God and see things from His perspective.

3. A Great Threat to the Kingdom Of Darkness

One day I had a vision of what I call the "strategy room of the enemy." In this vision, I saw a blackboard with bullet points on it. It was as if the enemy had written out directives in his fight against the Kingdom of Light. One of the bullet points said, **STOP INTERCESSION AT ALL COSTS.** If the enemy knows that the power of God is released in intercession, then it stands to reason that he would do anything to stop it. The enemy's strategy is to "shut down" intercession at all costs. Think in your own life of all the times the enemy has tried to keep you from prayer. Or, after you started praying, he would try to get you distracted so you would get frustrated and give up. The fact is, the devil hates prayer and will stop it if he can. I believe the enemy is very concerned when God's people pray. I believe this is the reason many prayer meetings are poorly attended and many people struggle in their individual prayer times. I refer to intercession as "God's secret weapon" because the enemy doesn't know what to do with intense, focused, powerful intercession. When God's people go before the throne and pray, God releases the resources of heaven that can't be stopped. The problem is, much of the church doesn't know what to do with intercession. If this is God's secret weapon, then why are a relative few people in the body of Christ involved?

"No one is a firmer believer in the power of prayer than the devil; not that he practices it, but he suffers from it." (Guy H. King)

4. It Brings Revival

There has never been a move of the Spirit, major or minor, that has happened without a strong connection to intercession. God moves on the hearts of men and women to call out to Him in prayer. That's what was happening just before the first Holy Spirit outpouring in the book of Acts. The believers were in one accord in prayer when the Spirit came in power. That has been the pattern ever since. There are those God has used mightily to intercede for revival. There are those like Frank Bartlerman who prayed for the Azuza Street outpouring. For years he had prayed five hours a day for a move of the Spirit. After a good while and no results, he asked the Lord if there was anything else he should do. The Lord said, "Yes, pray more." So he increased it to seven hours a day. There are those like Peggy and Christine Smith who gave themselves to intercession just prior to the Hebrides revival breaking out on the Isle of Lewis, Scotland. There are those like Evan Roberts and those with him when the Welsh revival broke out at Moriah Chapel. Interestingly, the Spirit came in the prayer chapel not the church sanctuary. And then more recently, the IHOP student awakening in Kansas City broke out just after the 10th anniversary of continuous night and day worship and intercession. We need to continue to pray for the outpouring of the Spirit as well as praying for the ultimate revival, the second coming of Christ.

Here are some quotes that I hope you find helpful:

David Yonggi Cho
"If you desire revival, there has never been, nor are there now, any short cuts to revival. The only key to revival is prayer."

R.A. Torrey
"There have been revivals without much preaching; but there has never been a mighty revival without mighty praying."

Selwyn Hughes
"Revival is a sovereign act of God in the sense that He alone can produce it, but it is transported to earth on the wings of fervent, believing prayer. Every revival in history – Pentecost included – began

in heaven, but flowed into the Church through the ramp of intercessory prayer."

The Global Prayer Movement

Ever since the early days of my walk with the Lord, I've had this attitude: whatever God is doing at any given time, I want to be a part of it. There was a season I spent time away from what He was doing. I was in some tributary, stuck in the mud, and I don't ever want to go there again. I believe God desires us to want to be involved in what He is doing. My time in the tributary was my fault. I hope I never go there again.

One of the main things God is doing today, which is happening at this very time, is a **global prayer movement**. This is something God is doing to prepare the world for what He's about to do. I'm determined that I want to be a part of it. I'm so excited about what God is doing in places like the International House of Prayer in Kansas City, 24-7 Prayer International, Burn 24/7 and thousands of houses of prayer being established around the world. There are prayer ministries like "The Call" with Lou Engle gathering people to pray. There are stadiums being the filled for the purpose of intercession in many nations throughout the world. God is also stirring His church to pray. Local churches are coming into a new emphasis of prayer. Will you please join me in determining that you also will be involved in what God is doing today? There is no need for you to be left out of the global prayer movement. These are very exciting days we are living in.

Here are some websites you might be interested in:
International House of Prayer Kansas City - www.ihopkc.org

24-7 Prayer International - www.24-7prayer.com
Burn 24/7- burn24-7.com
Lou Engle and The Call - www.thecall.com

5. It Is Foundational To Church Life

Intercession must not be seen as just a church department or a segment of the overall church ministry. Intercession is to be foundational for the entire functioning of the church. Every service, every department, every ministry, every outreach must be undergirded with intercessory prayer.

I love this story about Charles Spurgeon's "Boiler Room."
"Five young college students were spending a Sunday in London, so they went to hear the famed C.H. Spurgeon preach. While waiting for the doors to open, the students were greeted by a man who asked, 'Gentlemen, let me show you around. Would you like to see the heating plant of this church?' They were not particularly interested, for it was a hot day in July. But they didn't want to offend the stranger, so they consented. The young men were taken down a stairway, a door was quietly opened, and their guide whispered, 'This is our heating plant.' Surprised, the students saw 700 people bowed in prayer, seeking a blessing on the service that was soon to begin in the auditorium above. Softly closing the door, the gentleman then introduced himself. It was none other than Charles Spurgeon." (Our Daily Bread, April 24)

In the building of the local church, we should never become too busy or too focused on other things to make prayer a priority. Here an applicable quote from Pastor David Cho who just happens to be the pastor of the largest church in the world located in Seoul, Korea:

"You could remove the powerful preaching from our church and it would still continue. You could remove the administration of pastoral care through the cell group system/ and the church would still continue. But if you remove the prayer life of our church, it would collapse."

Is it any wonder that Jesus stayed up all night and prayed so that He could minister in the power of the Spirit all day the next day? If we want to have successful, growing, Holy Spirit empowered churches, there is no shortcuts to prayer. Everything must be bathed in prayer.

*"Be anxious for nothing, but **in everything by prayer** and supplication, with thanksgiving, let your requests be made known to God; and the peace of God, which surpasses all understanding, will guard your hearts and minds through Christ Jesus."* (Philippians 4:6-7)

"I have been driven many times to my knees by the overwhelming conviction that I had nowhere else to go." Abraham Lincoln

I personally learned this lesson the hard way a number of years back. My wife Darla and I were members of an outreach band in our church. She was one of the singers and I was the drummer. We had been asked to come and play at a park in another town. It was to be an evangelistic outreach, which most of our songs were geared towards. We had practiced weeks at a time, arranged for follow-up teams and promoted the concert throughout the community. It was to be a tremendous soul-winning event.

To our surprise we had about 200 people show up to listen to us. Everyone seemed to be enjoying the music. Then at the end, I got up to give an altar call. I delivered what I thought to be a stunning evangelistic message. Then an interesting thing happened…. **NOTHING.** When I asked for a show of hands, no one responded. So I gave another plea and still no one. Not knowing what else to do, I thanked everyone for coming and closed the concert. I was devastated. I was sure that there would be many that would come forward to receive the Lord.

The next day I went to the Lord in prayer. I asked Him if he could tell me why no one had responded to the altar call. He said, "If you had prayed one 10th of the time that you practiced your songs, I would have moved." I thought it over and realized that we did not pray for the event, not even once. I had to repent before the Lord for my presumption. Lesson learned.

I encourage you, especially if you're a church leader, to make prayer an emphasis in your church. Everything must be founded on an intercessory prayer culture. I would even challenge you to make intercessory prayer a part of every service, including Sunday morning. The enemy knows that he cannot stop a praying church because, for a praying church, the possibilities are limitless.

Final thought - These are just some of the reasons that intercession is so important. As we grasp the importance and value of intercession, we will be positioning ourselves to step into cooperation with the Holy Spirit to bring God's will into a living reality.

Chapter 2

CALLED TO PRAY
The Vision Changes

Youth Ministry! It was all my wife Darla and I could think of for 15 years. After pouring our lives into young people all that time, we were totally content and had no regrets. Then came a time that we believed God was calling us out of ministering to teenagers to something else. At the time we didn't even know what that something else was. It wasn't long before I began to get frustrated. All the areas of ministry I thought were going to open up for us didn't materialize. I was unaware of what God was really doing in this season. Instead of promotion, he was leading us into a season of deep testing. Then the question came. Was I really in this for Him, or for my own ministry ambitions? Ouch.

I remember being in a Friday night meeting getting ready to listen to a guest speaker that our church invited in. During worship I heard the Holy Spirit speak to my heart. He said, "You are frustrated aren't you?" I admitted I was. He said, "The reason you are so frustrated is that you don't have any vision for your life. I am planning to give you a new vision; and to prove that this is me talking to you right now, tonight he (the guest speaker) is going to talk about vision." I have always been one for a good confirmation, so I waited eagerly to see what was going to happen.

A few minutes later the guest speaker got up and the first words out of his mouth were, "Tonight I am going to talk about vision." I was very encouraged that God was about to give me another vision for my life and ministry. The only problem was that I thought when God said that He was going to give me a new vision, I assumed that He was going to do it that week. I was still unaware of some dross that had to come to the surface and some things still to walk through.

During the next year and a half or so I was ordained as an elder/pastor in the church and served faithfully during that season. Even though that was good, I knew there was something more that the Lord was calling me to.

Then in 1995 the vision came, but not in a way that I expected. We had just entered a time in our church where God had come in a powerful way. In every meeting He was there. I mean really there. I had never felt the presence of God in such a manner. I remember a time in the early 90s when the pastor would say during a Sunday morning service, "Isn't there a wonderful sense of God's presence here this morning." I would think to myself, "I don't feel anything; I must be really out of touch spiritually. I felt there must be something wrong with me." However, by 1995 that had all changed.

We spent hours and hours just soaking and basking in His glory. Many of us began to get real clarity in the Spirit. Visions and dreams were coming on a regular bases and it seemed that God was just as excited as we were. It was during one of the ministry times at the end of the service that I saw Jesus in a vision. He was standing over me as I lay on the floor. He said, **"Will you give your life for intercession?"** He had tears in His eyes when He said it and then He just looked at me. Then to confirm what God was saying, a sister came over and prayed for me. She said, "There is a strong Spirit of Intercession on you, brother." God was definitely speaking to me, so all I could do at that point was weep and say, "Yes Lord." It was a moment that changed the course of my whole life. The vision He had promised had come.

From that time on I did all I could to learn about intercession. But the most important lessons I learned were when I just began to pray.

An Impartation for Intercession

As I began to seek God about this new call on my life, one of the things I didn't realize is that I had yet to receive an impartation for intercession. When God calls, He always provides the enablement (dunimas power) to carry it out. I had a heart to be obedient to the word that came to me, but the thing I lacked was the power within to proceed forward.

That was a problem that was soon to be taken care of. God made it possible for my lifelong friend, Jeff Plueard, and I to attend the "Catch the Fire" conference in Toronto in October of 1995. The conference was awesome and God met us there in a powerful way. When we arrived I saw that they were going to have a workshop on intercession. I knew that I had to attend. Now when you have over 5000 people at a conference in a hotel, it gives the word 'workshop' a whole new meaning. There were at least 1000 people crammed in a hotel conference room that probably had seating for 600.

I was late in arriving and figured that there was no way I was even going to get in the door. While standing in the hallway wondering what to do, I noticed the man leading the workshop with a box full of handouts unable to enter the room as well. Then I had a (not totally selfless) idea. I would go over and ask the man if he wanted me to make a way for him to get into the workshop. I am a pretty big guy so I thought it might work. He said yes, so off we went. I blazed trail for the brother until we finally reached the front. There were people everywhere so the only place for me to sit was on the floor about 2 feet behind the podium.

The workshop was great and I learned a lot. But the real reason I was there was still to come. After the workshop, as people began to file out, I noticed that one of the ladies who had taught part of the workshop was praying for people. I thought since I was there I might just hang around and watch. Then this lady came over to me. She reminded me of the classic prayer warrior. She had a direct, no nonsense style. Then she looked at me sternly and said, "Well, what do you want?" Being caught off guard I said, "Uh, I don't know." She said, "Well do you want prayer?" I said, "Uh, yeah." She quickly put her hand on my stomach and I instantly doubled over and began to grown loudly. She then said, "Lord, give him the Spirit of Intercession in Jesus' name" and He did. The impartation had happened. I knew that God had touched me deep in my spirit and left a deposit there. Paul said in Romans 1:11, *"For I long to see you, that I may impart to you some spiritual gift, so that you may be established."*

I left that conference with something that I didn't have when I came. Often we think that when God asks us to do something, somehow we are to accomplish this in our own strength. Even Paul recognized his utter inability to carry out God's call on his life. He had great credentials, awesome drive and a sharp intellect. He had everything needed to be successful in this world. This is what he said about himself: ... *"though I also might have confidence in the flesh. If anyone else thinks he may have confidence in the flesh, I more so."* (Philippians 3:4) *"Yet indeed I also count all things loss for the excellence of the knowledge of Christ Jesus my Lord, for whom I have suffered the loss of all things, and count them as rubbish, that I may gain Christ."* (Philippians 3:8)

If Paul refused to trust in his own strength, should not we do the same? Many of us go to the place of prayer and feel as if we don't even know where to begin. God wants to empower us to pray. He wants to bring us to a place of intimacy with him. As we remain connected to the vine, He will give us the "Spirit of Intercession" that will enable us to pray with power and confidence.

An Unlikely Warrior

I remember in the 1960's as a kid, I had mixed feelings about war. I loved TV shows like Combat, 11 O'clock High, and McHale's Navy. These shows and others depicted some of the realities of World War II. On the other hand, the war in Vietnam that I was seeing on the nightly news completely and thoroughly soured me from wanting anything to do with warfare. I remember thinking that if the draft was still on when I became of age I might even head for Canada. I think some of this also came from the fact that I was quiet, reserved and mostly noncompetitive. It was as if I did not have anything in the natural that would make me a good soldier. I think many times it is an advantage not to have natural strength in that to which you are called. It allows us to know that what comes forth from us is of God and not ourselves.

When it comes to spiritual warfare, I think I must have been among the most unlikely people to do this. I also think that God loves taking the foolish and weak, the unexpected, to confound not just people, but the enemy as well.

Not long after receiving the initial call to intercession, the Lord also put a call on my life for spiritual warfare. This call came during another ministry time. Once again I had a vision while flat on my back on the floor with my eyes closed. In this vision I was standing with Jesus and He placed before me an old, well used, wooden chest. It was about 4 feet long, 30 inches wide and 30 inches high. I asked the Lord what was in the chest and He said, "These are your weapons." I instantly knew that along with intercession, He was calling me to spiritual warfare. He then opened the chest and inside was a rod, a sword and a bow with arrows. He asked me if I wanted to take a look at them, so I picked up the rod. I remember thinking that it was so cool that I could pull a six-foot rod out of four-foot chest. As I picked up the rod in the vision, in the natural my body shook violently as I lay on the floor. Then I put it back in the chest and the shaking subsided. It was the same as I held the other weapons. The next thing I saw in the vision was that I was surrounded by about four or five large warring angels. This one very strong and muscular looking angel slapped his hand on my shoulder and said in a deep voice, "Welcome, we will fight together." Feeling like the extremely green rookie on the team, I squeaked out some timid response like, "Yeah sounds great." Then the vision ended.

A few months later God spoke to me again about spiritual warfare. It was May of 1995. Some friends told me about this movie that had just come out called "Braveheart." It was a movie about Scotland and a man that I had never heard of named William Wallace. I decided to ask my dad if he would go and see the film with me. We have always shared a love for history and I thought he might enjoy it. As we were walking into the cinema I was surprised by something. I heard God speak to my heart and say, "I am going to show you what the severity of spiritual warfare is like." At the end of the first battle when William Wallace is shouting with his Claymore raised into the air, and the blood of the enemy all over his face, I knew that this was what God wanted me to see. We must understand something in this warfare. There is no neutral ground of negotiation with the enemy. Either you defeat him or he will defeat you. I was beginning to get the idea.

Then in October of that year, the Lord confirmed this calling at the "Catch the Fire" Conference in Toronto that I previously mentioned. I had already received the impartation for intercession as was determined that I was going to receive all that I could at this conference, so I went up for prayer after each session. It seemed that every time I was prayed for, the person would start with a simple blessing prayer, and then end up praying about God using me in warfare.

One night I was prayed for by one of the ministry team leaders. Upon seeing my conference name badge, his prayer went something like this, "Lord, bless Mike. Lord, touch Mike. Mike? Mike? Michael! Lord, teach him to fight like Michael the Archangel." Then I was overcome by the power of God and end up, yes you guessed it, back on the floor.

Since then I have discovered something interesting. God loves to place prophetic declarations about His intentions for us, even in simple things like our names. God takes a bit of time in scripture on properly naming people. I challenge you to look up the meanings of your names. I think you will be surprised at what you find there. I discovered that warfare was inherent in my very name. My first name Michael comes from "Michael the Archangel," who has the distinction of being the warring angel for Israel. One of the meanings of my middle name Keith is, "from the battlefield." Then the meaning of my last name, Bachelder, means, "young knight." Even in my youth, when there seemed to be nothing that would indicate warfare, God had already placed prophetic destiny in my name. He knew that someday I would answer this call.

Although I am still learning what it's like to be a warrior, and have made loads of mistakes along the way, I also consider this calling to be one of the greatest honors of my life. I give Jesus all glory and credit for any victory that I have had the privilege of being a part of. All praise to our great and victorious, warrior king.

High Profile Intercession

Not long after I received the impartation of the Spirit of Intercession, I heard there was going to be a Saturday morning intercession seminar at City Bible Church in Portland, Oregon. I gathered some of my friends from the church and off we went. The seminar was with South American evangelist Ed Silvoso, whom I had heard of but had never seen before. Right after worship the pastor gave an invitation for all *senior pastors* to come up and have Ed pray for them. This immediately brought a sigh of disappointment, as I was only an associate pastor at the time. So all the *senior pastors* came up and the rest of us watched as the *senior pastors* were prayed for by the man of God. Can you tell that, by this time, my attitude was really starting to sour? I began to whine under my breath, "Why is it always the *senior pastors* who get all the good prayer? Why can't they just say pastors instead of *senior pastors?*" To make matters worse, I looked over to the prayer line again and saw a friend of mine talking to Ed Silvoso. He was a missionary to Bosnia and not a *senior pastor.* So Ed started praying for him. I said to myself, "That brother is going for the blessing." So I headed right over there and was hit with a brilliant idea. I would go over and help pray for my friend and then Ed would see me standing there and move over and pray for me. So I initiated my foolproof plan. The only problem was that when Ed was done praying, the pastor leading the meeting came and grabbed Ed and took him to the other end of the prayer line to pray for another *senior pastor* who had just arrived. Then I really began to snivel. "It's just not fair. After all I…" In mid-sentence the Holy Spirit interrupted me. I had honestly forgotten all about Him. He said, "Excuse me, but can I ask you a question?" My heart sank and I knew immediately that I was being convicted about my bad attitude. **"Are you here for him or are you here for Me?"** At that point I was spiritually busted. I said, "Oh Lord, please forgive me, I'm sorry. I'm here for You." "Assume the position then," was his response. I knew intuitively that what He meant was to stand there as if someone was going to pray for me. So I stood there with no one around me. I raised my hands and closed my eyes and was hit by the power of God. I immediately fell to the floor with no one to catch me. It was okay though; I didn't feel a thing. The Holy Spirit was all over me. It was incredible.

After a while the Lord spoke to me again and told me to sit up that He wanted to show you something. As I sat up, He asked me, "When you walked into the room this morning, did anybody notice you?" I said, "No, not really." He continued, "When Ed Silvoso walked in, do you think anybody noticed him?" I quickly thought of our little group who were seated together at the beginning of the meeting. I think it was I who pointed him out to everyone. I said to the Lord, "Yes, a lot of people noticed when he walked in." "Do you want to know what the difference is?" He asked. "He is a high profile person and you are a low profile person." I fully agreed with that. "I have an offer for you." He said. **"How would you like to be low profile in the natural, but high profile in the realm of the Spirit?"** All of a sudden the full import of what He was saying flooded my thoughts. Scriptures began to fill my mind like; *"And the evil spirit answered and said, "Jesus I know, and Paul I know; but who are you?"* (Acts 19:15) and *"Therefore humble yourselves under the mighty hand of God, that He may exalt you in due time."* (1 Peter 5:6)

In response to his question, I said, "Yes, I'll take that." I knew that it meant that being recognized as a person of prayer in the spirit realm would be more important than being recognized as a "High Profile" person in the earthly realm. Although I knew that there are those that God has called to be both, for me the one was just fine. How fortunate we are when God gives us a chance to see if we really "get it" when it comes to what He is trying to teach us.

A while later I was back at City Bible Church for their first Intercession conference. During one of the ministry times one of the guest speakers, Claudio Friedson, was making his way through the crowd praying for people as he went. He was about twenty feet away when I saw him. I immediately turned away, lifted my hands and said, "Lord, I just want You to know that I am here for You and no one else." Just a few seconds later, Claudio went about twenty feet out of his way to come and pray for me. He quickly looked at my nametag and said, "Lord, bless Mike." The next second, I was on the floor with God's presence all over me and my heart was overwhelmed with thankfulness.

Intercession – A Prophetic Journey

Much of what I learned came as I attempted to glean from the life of others who have gone before me in their own journeys of prayer. I've read books, listened to loads of teaching tapes and CDs (and now MP3's), and asked questions as much as I could. However, the most important lessons I learned came as I just asked the Lord as the disciples did, "Lord, teach me to pray."

You may say to yourself, "I am not even sure I can hear Gods voice clearly. How could I possibly ask Him to teach me anything?" I have found that if I just step out to do it, I begin to hear Him before I even realize it. The key is, are you desperate to hear Him? I found out that I hear God much clearer in the midst of a difficult time than when all is going well.

I remember a time in youth ministry when everything was going fine, then it all seemed to be going south fast. We began to have trouble with a lot of the young people. Even our leadership kids were having bad attitudes and getting tripped up. It all came to a head at one of our infamous "all-nighters." Between the dirty jokes, rebellious attitudes and sneaking off, there came a point that we knew something had to change. So we asked God if there was anything He wanted us to do differently. He responded by giving us a whole new strategy for youth ministry, one that actually worked. The key is, we must be desperate for Him. Like Moses declared to Israel, *"But from there you will seek the LORD your God, and you will find Him if you seek Him with all your heart and with all your soul."* (Deuteronomy 4:29)

God wants to reveal truth to us, but often we are too busy, too impatient and too proud to ask Him. As a person of prayer you are in a training process. God always wants to teach you something. Intercession isn't just about praying to get a prayer answered. It's also about teaching us along the way. It is not just learning how to intercede but learning the heart of God; how He thinks, how He feels and how He is.

As I was praying one day, the Lord led me into some rather heavy intercession. The more I prayed the more burdened I became. I could sense the passion of God, as well as the fear of God. Then He said to me "Do you want to know how I feel?" For the next few minutes I stood trembling as the God of the universe told me not only what He thinks, but also how He feels. It was an amazing and fearsome time. You see, God will often tell someone what He thinks, but seldom does He declare how He feels.

The more you get to know Him, the more you will find that He will want to share things with you. I have heard of people who say, "I never have visions or dreams Why don't I see things in the Spirit?" Part of the answer is directly related to the time and energy you put into seeking after God. In Deuteronomy 4:29, the Hebrew word for **seek** is **da^rash**. This means to *"pursue frequently."* (Strong's) God will often wait to see if we are serious about finding Him. It would seem that as we have the same heart as David did, we will find God in the place where He dwells. Listen to David's heart as he seeks after God. *"O God, You are my God; Early will I seek You; My soul thirsts for You; My flesh longs for You in a dry and thirsty land where there is no water."* (Psalms 63:1) *"My soul follows close behind You; Your right hand upholds me.* (Psalms 63:8)

The Hebrew word for **hard** is *"da^baq"* which means, *"catch by pursuit."* (Strong's) To be involved in high profile intercession, you must go after God. It seems that many of us have adopted an American, microwave, remote control attitude towards prayer. If it's not self-serving, instant and quickly changeable we don't want it. God's plan is self-denying, He takes his time and He never changes. But His way is always the best way. In intercession you must do it His way.

Called Aside to Pray

Many of us thrive on being right in the middle of what God is doing at any given time. We shudder to think that God would ever set us "on the shelf" for any reason. We are convinced that the pruning process of John 15:2 doesn't apply to us. We may have the thought that the only direction for us is upwards. "After all, God really needs me to do all this stuff I am doing. What would He do without me? He understands I have an important ministry."

Now we may not say it quite that way, but it might be what we believe deep in our hearts. We are in a season where we must understand that God is going after all of our selfish ambition, self-promotion and glorying in title and position. Now it is okay to have a title or position as long as your heart is right in relationship to that position. Here is a verse that I have endeavored to base my life and ministry on, and I have found that it works. Proverbs 18:16 says, *"A man's gift makes room for him, and brings him before great men."*

Albert Barnes in his commentary, Notes on the Bible, speaks of the word "gift" this way: *the "gift" (or, bribe), by a bold personification, appears as the **powerful "friend at court,"** who introduces another, and **makes him welcome in high places**.*

I have seen this verse activated in my life many times as God has allowed me to spend time with people I never imagined I would spend time with. We need to understand that if we are trying to open our own doors, the hand of God is stayed from opening them for us. Many times I have tried to make room for my gift, instead of letting my gift make room for me. Instead of letting Jesus be my **"friend at court,"** I have chosen to represent myself in the matter of ministry advancement. By taking the reins of my own life and ministry, I am actually telling God that I don't really trust Him to open the right doors at the right times. What we must understand is that the Father is taking the emphasis off our identity being based on what we do, to a basis of just knowing Him.

Am I saying that we are not to do anything? Not at all. What I am saying is that everything we do in our service to Him must be founded on our knowing Him. It's important to see that God cares much more for us than He does our ministry? That is why prayer is so vital to us. It brings us to the place of knowing Jesus. In my own life, when this word about intercession came to me, I was very busy **doing** for God. I was an associate pastor in charge of many different areas of the church, as well as being the main drummer on the worship team. There always seemed to be more to be done than I had time to do it. So I tried to add prayer to my to-do list, but it didn't work very well. During a prophetic conference we had with Wes and Stacy Campbell in 1996, God gave me this prophetic word through Stacy that helped put things in perspective:

*"I just feel that you have done many things in the kingdom of God and that it is not just this one or this one, but that you have done sort of everything. And I feel like in a very positive sense you have been a jack of all trades. You can do this and you can do this and you can do that, but I feel the Spirit that is coming on you is **primarily for intercession**. I feel there is a strong intercessory thing that God is trying to build in you, but I feel like it's just beginning compared to what it is going to be like. And that intercession is what God is calling you to. He is calling you from doing many things to begin to focus. And I think this is going to be a struggle for you because you've done so many things. And you are used to doing a little bit of this and a little bit of that, but I feel God is putting a hook in your mouth and drawing you to the prayer closet, because you are to be mighty though God to the pulling down of strongholds and that this anointing is an intercessory anointing for you. And God is looking for someone to take on His burden. And the Lord says, you have taken on My burdens, but now God wants you to **pray, pray, pray.**"* Although this word was for me, I believe God wants you to pray, pray, pray, pray as well.

Final thought - God is looking for people who will allow their lives to be "**set aside**" for the purpose of prayer. He is looking for people who will take up His burden and come into the throne room to intercede. However, instead of looking at it as being set aside, it is really an invitation to be **called up** to where He is. It is an absolutely incredible invitation.

Chapter 3

INTERCESSION AND CHARACTER

I n this chapter, I would like to look at the process that God uses to work His character in us. It is the deep working of the Holy Spirit in us that prepares the way for the pure and powerful flow of intercession through us. God is just as concerned with the integrity of the vessel as He is about that which dwells in the vessel. (2 Timothy 2:21) Now am I saying that you can't be used in intercession until you have flawless character? No, God can use you as soon as you surrender your life to Him. What we need to do is recognize that what God allows us to go through is His means of working His character in us. The principle is this, **God's work in us is more important than God's work through us.**

"PRAYER governs conduct and conduct makes character. Conduct is what we do; character is what we are. Conduct is the outward life. Character is the life unseen, hidden within, yet evidenced by that which is seen. Conduct is external, seen from without; character is internal -- operating within. In the economy of grace, conduct is the offspring of character. Character is the state of the heart, conduct its outward expression. Character is the root of the tree, conduct, the fruit it bears." (E.M. Bounds)

"If the foundations are destroyed, What can the righteous do? The LORD is in His holy temple, The LORD's throne is in heaven; His eyes behold, His eyelids test the sons of men. The LORD tests the righteous,

but the wicked and the one who loves violence His soul hates." (Psalms 11:3-5)

"…working itself into your conduct as God accurately reproduces his character in you." (Ephesians 4:24 The Message)

"Being confident of this very thing, that He who has begun a good work in you will complete it until the day of Jesus Christ." (Philippians 1:6)

This is Only a Test

Many of us, as we begin to walk with God, wonder why He doesn't shield us from going through difficult and unpleasant circumstances. In my early days of ministry, I experienced an extremely difficult time that left me hurt, disillusioned, and confused. I couldn't understand how God would allow all this to happen. As I desperately prayed to find some answer for all that I was experiencing, I finally heard the voice of God speak, cutting through all the confusion. He said, "Son, this is the only way that I could get you to where I want you to be." Then I began to understand. If it were left up to me, I would usually take the path of least resistance. God not only has His ways of directing our lives, but it is in the "going through" that God shapes us into the image of Jesus. (James 1:2-4, Philippians 1:6) It is in the testing that God is accomplishing the purifying work in us to make us vessels that He can move through. In intercession, this is important because it is required that we pray the heart of God, not our own desires. Intercession must have the ingredient of selflessness to be effective. This is only one of the many attributes of God that He wants to work in us. The way it is accomplished is by the testing of the Lord. The life of Joseph is one of the clearest examples of testing in the life of a believer.

*"He sent a man before them --- Joseph --- who was sold as a slave. They hurt his feet with fetters, He was laid in irons. Until the time that his word came to pass, **the word of the LORD tested him.**"* (Psalms 105:17-19)

The Lord had arranged for Joseph to be tested to prepare him for all that He had called him to. Joseph could have pleaded to God for an easier way, but he didn't. No, he held to the path that God had placed before him. A huge help in getting through the testing is just realizing that it is a test. When you are armed with this revelation, you can see what God is doing. Then you can quickly submit, get on with it, pass it and move forward. It's when you are in the midst of the difficulty and don't know what is happening that confusion, bitterness and blame-shifting come in. Another danger is to think we have reached a place where we have been through all of our testing and we are now free of such things happening to us.

I remember having breakfast with a young evangelist who was beginning to build a prominent ministry and was in high demand. I knew he had been saved for about seven years and I believed God wanted me to let him know that there was some testing still ahead for him. As I told him this, his response was to sit back in his chair and say, "Well I appreciate the prophetic warning brother, but I'll have you know that I have already been through all my testing." I responded with an "okay" and left it at that. It's not that the brother wasn't anointed and that he didn't have a legitimate ministry from the Lord. But I believed

47

God wanted him to understand that in order to reach his full potential, surrender to God's inner work was required.

In many ways our testing will continue until the time we as an individual will enter eternity. I once had the privilege of having dinner with a man named Arthur Burt. At the time he was 95 years old and had been in the ministry for 60+ years. This man was a friend and disciple of Smith Wigglesworth. He told me that he had just been through a season of God challenging and testing him in certain areas of his life. I remember thinking, "Oh great, this is never going to end, is it?" Arthur made it clear that even after living 95 years he was still a work in progress.

I had the privilege of learning a great lesson about character from Arthur when I went to hear him speak at a pastor's meeting. After he finished He asked if anyone had any questions. No one responded so we ended the meeting and had lunch. During lunch, I thought of a question to ask him. I said, "Arthur, I do have a question? How does someone go years in the ministry without going bad in the end?" I have known several leaders who had a great beginning but did not end well.

So I thought I would ask Arthur for some insight. He said something that I did not expect. He said, "You answer me this, what do you have to do to a piece of fruit for it to go bad?" Before I could say anything he answered the question. He said "Absolutely nothing." I assume by the look on my face it was obvious that I was not getting his drift. So he continued, "The fruit was made by God to be taken and absorbed into the body. The second you begin to be **more than just another part of the**

body you will begin to go bad." All of a sudden all the lights came on and I understood what he was saying. He finished with, "We are all like keys on a piano. We only truly shine when our key is touched by the Master, the rest of the time we are just one of the keys on His piano."

The test of God is that which will bring us into a proper understanding of who we are in relationship to the Lord and His body. This is God's work to conform us to the image of His son. (Romans 8:29)

Here are some of the specific tests that God has designed for us to go through to bring us along in character so we can be effective in intercession. Though there are many more particular kinds of tests, we will look at some of the most valuable ones:

1. The Test of Time

When we receive a revelation of what God has called us to, in the immediate something very interesting happens; **nothing**. We often automatically assume that when the Lord speaks to us about our future He is talking about next week or next month. Then as the months and sometimes years go by, we begin to wonder what is going on. Did we not hear the Lord properly? Did God, for some reason, change His mind? Is "this or that" keeping me from my destiny? Often this leads us to go to the Lord frustrated and asking questions about what is taking so long. God wants to make sure that we don't give up on what He has spoken because of impatience. In James 1:2 we are admonished to, *"Count it all joy when you fall into various trials, knowing that the **proving of your faith** works **patience"***.

Remember the principle: **God's work in us is more important than God's work through us**. It is based on what God knows and what we don't know. There are timing issues, preparation issues, maturity issues, all kinds of things that factor into the fulfillment of the word. Many of the Bible greats such as Abraham, Joseph, Moses, David and Paul had to go through this test. Are we willing to wait on His timing?

2. The Test of Recognition

Matthew 6:5 *"...and when you pray, you shall not be like the hypocrites. For they love to pray standing in the synagogues and in the corners of the streets, **so that they may be seen by men**. Truly I say to you, they have their reward."*

This test goes right after that which dwells in us as a part of our sin nature, the need for recognition and approval. Actually, our whole society is based on it. From sports to entertainment or from academics to the arts, we are expected to "perform" and "show our worth." From a young age we learn to say, "Look at me. See what I can do." I don't think this is necessarily all bad, but as we begin to walk with the Lord, if we don't submit this attitude to Him, it can trip us up.

Before I was a believer I had a great desire to find out what my "identity" was. I was the middle kid of four brothers and a sister, and the only one yet to achieve recognition in anything. When I would meet people they would say, "Hey, aren't you *Ken-Steve-Dave-Barb's* brother?" Then at the age of seventeen, I thought I had found it. I bought an old red sparkle drum kit and began to play. I found that I had some natural talent in drums, so I threw myself into learning to play.

After a while I felt I was good enough to call myself by my newly-acquired title, "Drummer." There was a sense that I had at least found something I was good at. But true fulfillment didn't come until about a year later when I was given a new title, that of "Child of God." In the first year of my salvation I found my new life in Christ was setting me free from much of the drive to prove myself. But I did find myself enjoying the recognition as an on-fire believer. I threw myself into prayer and reading the word, wanting all of God that I could get. Upon finishing the New Testament, I said to myself, "Well I have read that book, now what do I do?" I came to the conclusion that the only logical next step was to start memorizing scripture. So as I began to memorize the various chapters in the New Testament, word got out that I really knew the Bible, and I liked the attention. Then I arrived at my big opportunity to "show off" my great accomplishment. I was asked during a Bible study to read a certain passage. As my good fortune would have it, it was a verse that I had memorized. So with a smile on my face I abruptly closed my Bible and proceeded to recite the verse.

As I started to speak, to my immediate embarrassment, the Lord extracted the verse from my memory. With a red face I clumsily fumbled in my Bible to find the verse. God is going to give us plenty of opportunity to shine. But will it be for our glory or His? Like Paul said in 2 Corinthians 10:17, *"he who glories, let him glory in the LORD."*

3. The Test of Promotion

1 Samuel 2:7, *"GOD brings poverty and GOD brings wealth; he lowers, he also lifts up."* (The Message)

A good indicator that we are being challenged by this test is when we think we have a right to some position or title. We often like to apply the world's means of promotion to our life and ministry. But once again, God's ways are not our ways. In the world things such as seniority, ambition, dedication, skill and flattery is what get a person promoted. The key is making a good impression on the person doing the promoting. If you work hard and prove your worth, you will get ahead. If we overlay this template in our ministry situations, we will have problems. Our first one will be in trying to impress the person over us. Often this is the Pastor or some other leader. We might think that if we approach this politically, it will work. Wrong. **We must understand that true promotion comes from the Lord.** He will then channel it through designated authority but it comes from Him.

The next problem comes in when someone else is promoted and we think it should be us. For example, let's say the Pastor decided to put someone in charge of intercession in the church and he gives the position to another brother or sister. We might say, "Who do they think they are? After all, I am more qualified than they are. I have more gifting and I have been here longer. I have also been doing all I can to prove to the Pastor that I am the best one for the position. I guess maybe I should leave and go somewhere I will be used and appreciated." No, you shouldn't leave. You should stay and realize God is testing you and you need to submit to the process. Paul is very clear in Galatians 5:26, *"That means we will not compare ourselves with each other as if one of us were better and another worse. We have far more interesting things to do with our lives. Each of us is an original."* (The Message) Romans 12:10 says, *"Be kindly affectionate one to another with brotherly love; in honor **preferring one another."*** In 1 Peter 5:6, Peter chimes in, *"Humble yourselves therefore under the mighty hand of God, that he may exalt you in due time."*

We need to come to the place we are fine with promotion and we are also okay with lack of promotion. As long as it is what God wants, it is alright. I know that sometimes this test comes with strong emotions of being treated unfairly or unjustly. This is a time to trust His grace and draw close to the Father and He will get you through it. It is in this place of trust that we can rest in the knowledge that we have already been promoted to the highest position possible, which is the grand title of son or daughter of the Most High God.

4.   The Test of Ambition

The Oxford dictionary definition of ambition is this: *"strong desire to do or achieve something, desire for success, wealth or fame."* This word had its origin in the practice of Roman candidates for office, who went about the city to solicit votes. Not all ambition is wrong. There are many things in life that people go after and achieve and we honor them for that. But what we are referring to in this test is what the Bible calls **selfish ambition.**

Paul speaks of in this way, *"The former insincerely preach Messiah from **selfish ambition**, thinking that they add affliction to my chains."* (Philippians 1:16) *"Let nothing be done through selfish ambition or conceit, but in lowliness of mind let each esteem others better than himself."* (Philippians 2:3) Then James goes even a bit deeper, *"But if you have bitter jealousy and **selfish ambition** in your heart, don't boast and don't lie against the truth."* (James 3:14) *"For where jealousy and **selfish ambition** are, there is confusion and every evil deed."* (James 3:16)

One of the most important character defects that God is going after in His people today is selfish ambition. The drive within us to succeed, achieve and accomplish that which we have vision for. The linchpin of ambition is our motive. What makes us sacrifice our time, energy and, often times, finances to see our vision accomplished? What is actually in our hearts as a motivation?

This is the main thought in Hebrews 4:12, *"For the word of God is quick, and powerful, and sharper than any two-edged sword, piercing even to the dividing asunder of soul and spirit, and of the joints and marrow, and is a **discerner of the thoughts and intents of the heart"**.* The test of ambition is to reveal to us the true motive (thoughts and intents) of the actions we take and the words we say. Though it may all look good on the outside, God judges our heart. The Lord wants our service to be pure, not mixed with our own self-seeking ambition. If we go the way of ambition, we can produce for a while, but in the long run ultimately we lose. William Shakespeare said it this way:

"Cromwell, I charge thee, fling away ambition;
By that sin fell the angels. How can man then,
The image of his maker, hope to win by it."

When it comes to the whole area of selfish ambition, the Lord put it to me like this, "I want your life to be like a well that others can draw living water from. The well first must be dug and the debris that is removed is all of your selfish ambition." He wants a pure stream coming forth from us to bring life to others. He wants us to intercede based on His agenda, not our own. So in this test, it is the piercing light of the Word that brings the Spirit of truth to bear on any gray areas of ambition in us. Then by His kindness, He leads us to repentance.

I see selfish ambition as one of the scourges of the twenty first century western church. How many church splits, troubles and devastation have this evil at its root? In our society we honor, praise and glorify people for their ambition to accomplish great things. We show them great respect for their ability to "make it happen" in the realm of earthly achievement. Now this is not all bad, however when you try to apply the same thought in the context of kingdom, things can get sticky. In this test God is after not just what we do, but the motor that drives us to do it. The intents of the heart are what He is after. He wants to be our sole motivation for all we do for Him, and His power the motor. He has ordained us for good works, but He wants those works to be motivated by love.

Sometimes I think we have heard 1 Corinthians 13 so much that we forget that most of the chapter deals with motive. A love relationship with Jesus is the key to living after His heart instead of our own. Jesus said, *"for without me you can do **nothing.**"* (John15:5) The word "**nothing**" in this verse comes from the Greek word, "**ouedis**." The word literally means "not even one", which infers that we can do nothing of eternal significance without being totally dependent on Him. So it seems selfish ambition has to go or all we will have left is hay, wood, and stubble. We must allow the Holy Spirit to deal with us in this area so we can move into the "greater works" that He has called us to.

5. The Test of Achievement

As I began to write about this test, I had just returned from a prayer hike. While walking through the woods near our house in Gartcosh, Scotland, the Holy Spirit led me into a time of prayer, repentance and healing. He had spoken to me about something that had developed in my heart as a young man.

I grew up in Western Oregon as the number three son of a mother who was raised on a ranch in Idaho and a dad who was a bona fide lumberjack. My dad was a timber faller for Weyerhauser Company in the 1950s, 60s, and 70s. He was one of the best loggers that Oregon has ever seen. I grew up loving the outdoors. Much of my childhood was spent hiking, fishing, camping and anything else to do with just being outside. One of the things that we loved to do as a family was to go deer hunting. And yes, my mother was as good a hunter, or better, than any of us.

I loved hunting as a boy, and though I don't do it as much these days, I still think it's great. However, as I became a young man, something happened in my heart that changed how I approached the time I spent hunting. Somehow I adopted a prideful need to achieve to prove to my friends, and I guess myself, that I was a good hunter. That drive to achieve caused me to do whatever it took to bag the big one. It was no longer about just being in the outdoors and having a great time, it was about trying to prove something.

That morning as I was on my hike, the Holy Spirit revealed that I had never truly repented of this heart attitude. As I walked through the issue with the Holy Spirit, I felt a great release come. Then to top it off, as I finished the prayer, a deer walked out of the woods onto the trail and stopped to look at me. I was overcome with the love and goodness of God for setting me free. It is a wonderful thing to walk free of the selfish drive to achieve.

Now, am I saying that it is wrong to achieve things in life? Of course not. What I am saying is that God wants us to be free from the drive to achieve that is rooted in our carnal nature, fueled by a performance mentality. This is a bit different than the test of ambition. This deals with the idea that our worth and value in life is based on what we achieve. God wants us to know that no matter what we are able to do for Him, it is only as we are enabled by grace that we can do it. Bill Johnson said it this way, *"Poor in spirit is that place of humility where you realize everything comes simply as a gift of grace."* (From the message, "The Enemy Within")

That which we do achieve in the kingdom should not be based on our ability, but on the peaceful, joyful, satisfying life connection with God that we have. Jesus referred to this connection in John 15:5. *"I am the Vine; you are the branches. He who abides in Me, and I in him, bears much fruit; for without Me you can do nothing."*

It is out of our knowing of Him that we can achieve fruit in this life that is lasting, worthwhile and ultimately eternal. Jesus brought His point home in some of what I consider the most sobering verses of the New Testament. I can still feel the "ouch" in Matthew 7:21-23. *"Not everyone who says to Me, 'Lord, Lord,' shall enter the kingdom of heaven, but he who does the will of My Father in heaven. Many will say to Me in that day, 'Lord, Lord, have we not prophesied in Your name, cast out demons in Your name, and done many wonders in Your name?' And then I will declare to them, 'I never knew you; depart from Me, you who practice lawlessness!'"*

Now it wasn't what these people achieved that was wrong, it was that they achieved it without knowing Him that was wrong. Knowing always comes before doing. In intercession one of the things we have to deal with is the fact that often we will never know until heaven what was achieved by our prayers. We must come to a place where that is all right with us.

These five tests are by no means the only ones that God has arranged for us, but the good news is that they are all "open book" and He promises to be with us every step of the way.

Revelation by the River

In the building of character, it is not as much about God removing the negative from us, as it is about him imparting the positive into us. Many of us have a great hunger to "go deep" in the things of God. Although this is God's heart for us, we must first allow Him to "go deep" in us and root out those issues that have become obstacles to us. This is why the ministry of (Holy Spirit led) inner healing is so important.

This is how the Lord put it to me one day while I was praying by the McKenzie River in Oregon. (This was during a time when God was moving and many were talking about being "in the river" of God's presence.) He said, "Look at that tree by the river bank." As I looked I saw a tree that was standing but barely hanging on the bank by its roots. Then he said to me, "If you want to be in the river you need to be prepared to have your roots exposed. When this happens, if you respond correctly, I will, as the husbandman, come and shore up your roots and you will remain a strong tree planted by the river. If you harden your heart instead of responding, the tree will fall." As he spoke I was shaking in the fear of the Lord.

The interesting thing was that the very next time I went to the river to pray, a few days later, that same tree had fallen into the river, barely hanging on to the bank by its roots. Then the next time I went to that place, that tree was gone, washed downstream. Now the exposing I believe He was talking about isn't necessarily to people. It is when the Lord reveals our heart to us, we must respond and allow Him to work a deep work in us. David said in Psalms 26:2, "*Examine me, O LORD, and prove* me; **try** *my mind and my heart.*" The word try is the Hebrew word **tsâraph** which means, *"To fuse metal, that is, refine, cast, founder, goldsmith, melt, pure, purge away, try."* (Strong's) In Isaiah 48:10 the Lord talks about bringing us through this process. *"Behold, I have refined you, but not as silver;* **I have tested you** *in the furnace of affliction."*

Vessels of Honor

For a long time, I couldn't figure out how to reconcile the idea of being a broken vessel and being a vessel of honor. Then one day it hit me. If we will **allow brokenness** to lead us to the Healer, then **He will mend us** and transform us into vessels of honor for His glory.

Brokenness + Mending = Vessel of Honor

In Mark 14:3, we read about a woman coming to Jesus with an alabaster box. She broke the box and poured the ointment on the head of Jesus, releasing a great fragrance into the room. To have the true fragrance and anointing of Christ operating through us, we must allow the breaking to happen. Brokenness not only releases the anointing, but **it qualifies us to operate in the anointing**. Ultimately it is God himself who is the author of the breaking process. I came across some interesting verses. In Hosea 6:1 it says, *"Come and let us return to the Lord.* **For He has torn, and He will heal us; He has stricken, and He will bind us up.**" Psalms 51:8 says, *"**Make me hear joy and gladness, that the bones You have broken may rejoice.**"*

At first it offended my religious mind to think that God Himself was allowing my brokenness. We need to come to the place where we truly believe God is in control and that He knows what He is doing. Graham Cook said it this way, *"God allows in his wisdom what he could easily prevent by his power."* Our brokenness isn't an accident but it is by design.

I remember being at a conference that had two different men singing a special song. The first night one brother sang and the anointing was so powerful that there was hardly a dry eye in the place. The next night another brother sang who was equally talented musically, but when he sang the anointing was flat. In my curiosity I asked the Lord, "What was the difference between these two brothers?" He said at one word, "Brokenness." It appeared to me that one brother had allowed God to work deep in his life and sanctify his gift. The other brother had not. Ultimately it is the divine work of brokenness that qualifies us for the anointing.

Brokenness is that which, if we will allow it, brings us closer to Him. Psalms 34:18 says, *"The **LORD is near** to those who have a broken heart, and saves such as have a contrite spirit."* Then in Philippians 3:10, *"that I may **know Him** and the power of His resurrection, and the fellowship of His sufferings, being conformed to His death."* As we cooperate with this process of brokenness, we will be transformed into vessels of honor. (2 Timothy 2:21)

In Isaiah 64:8 we read, **"But now, O LORD, You are our Father; we are the clay, and You our potter; And all we are the work of Your hand."** One of the main keys to building the character of Jesus is just staying on the potter's wheel long enough for Him to shape us. Often at a crucial point in the molding we want jump off the wheel and do it our way for a while. I challenge you to stay on the wheel and let God make you into a vessel of honor He can move through mightily in intercession.

Obstacles or Opportunities

An obstacle is *"a thing that blocks one's way or hinders progress."* (Oxford) When we refer to someone's "walk with God," we are talking about their life journey on the straight and narrow path. Obstacles are that which attempts to slow, hinder and, if possible, stop our growth and progress as believers. These could be good things in our lives, not just bad. They could be big walls, or small stones we trip over. Everything, has the potential to be an obstacle, from secret sin to "good" things that nobody would seem to question, this idea is put forth in 2 Timothy 2:3-4, *"You therefore must endure hardship as a good soldier of Jesus Christ. No one engaged in warfare entangles himself with the affairs of this life, that he may please him who enlisted him as a soldier."*

The Hebrew word for "entangles" is "empleko" which means *"to entwine."* There are many things in life that we can get wrapped up in. If it hinders our walk with Jesus, it must be brought into question and examined. Even the little things can trip us up. After all, it is the little foxes that spoil the vine. (Song of Solomon 2:15)

Hold what you value with an open hand. If you try to possess it with a firm grasp, it will slip through your fingers. I read this prophetic word from Marsha Burns that I thought was fitting: *"The earth is Mine and all that is in it, says the Lord. You cannot own what does not belong to you, and I continue to establish the concept of stewardship and not ownership in the hearts of My people. You, beloved, are only sojourners on the earth, not permanent residents. Your earthly existence is but for a moment. Keep eternal perspective. Let go, and yield to the work and moving of My Spirit."* (From Small Straws in A Soft Wind by Bill and Marsha Burns. A daily prophetic blog)

Stumbling Blocks or Stepping Stones

There are two kinds of obstacles in our lives: the ones that need to be removed, and the ones that God is allowing to be in our path to work something in us. Let's allow the ones that remain to be an opportunity for us to rise up and turn them into stepping stones in our walk with God.

This was Paul's attitude in 2 Corinthians 12:7-10, *"And lest I should be exalted above measure by the abundance of the revelations, a thorn in the flesh was given to me, a messenger of Satan to buffet me, lest I be exalted above measure. Concerning this thing I pleaded with the Lord three times that it might depart from me. And He said to me, "My grace is sufficient for you, for My strength is made perfect in weakness. Therefore, most gladly I will rather boast in my infirmities, that the power of Christ may rest upon me. Therefore, I take pleasure in infirmities, in reproaches, in needs, in persecutions, in distresses, for Christ's sake. For when I am weak, then I am strong."*

We must realize there is abundant grace for any obstacle that we face and that ultimately we must see obstacles as opportunities.

What Is It Really All About?

What the issue is really all about is God bringing me as an individual to **the end of myself.** This is the idea behind 2

Corinthians 4:7, *"…but we have this treasure in earthen vessels that the excellence of the power may be of God and not of us."*

I had a vision that demonstrates this point. In the vision I was walking on a dry, rocky trail that I sensed had been very hard to walk. As I walked along, I came to a line across the trail, and written on my side of the line were the words, **END OF SELF**. As I stood before this line I heard the Lord speak into my spirit. He said, "Will you cross this line?" I knew in the vision that I had come to a place where I had nothing left to hold on to. So I said to the Lord. "Yes I will. What have I got to lose?" As I stepped across the trail, it turned from a dusty, rocky trail to a path made of pure gold. It was like being in a place where the mysteries are revealed. Every direction I would look I would see a new facet of God and the wonders of His kingdom. It was also a place of instant answers to prayer. I would say, "Lord I need…" and I would have it before I could finish the sentence. It was a place of total communion and intimacy with the Lord. I believe what God was showing me was not just heaven, but a place in the Spirit that we can live in now.

If we are going to be effective in intercession, or anything in the kingdom for that matter, this is the place we must live. Jesus said, *"He who finds his life shall lose it. And he who loses his life for My sake shall find it."* (Matthew 10:39)

Dealing with Heart Issues

When we talk about God working in our character, what we are really referring to is allowing him to deal with our heart issues.

*"Keep your heart with all diligence, for out of it
spring the issues of life."* (Proverbs 4:23)

The Holy Spirit wants to bring us to a place where He can remove those things in our lives that are continually tripping us up and impeding our forward progress. Sometimes the issues are blatantly obvious to us, and other times we don't seem to have a clue they are there. Either we don't see, them or we choose not to see them, especially when our issues are connected to past wounds and hurts. We must allow the Holy Spirit to move deep within us to bring healing, wholeness and restoration. If we do not allow the Spirit to touch our issues, we can easily become wounded people who wound other people.

The Lord gave me a picture of what can cause such wounding. I saw a picture of a brother with a shield strapped to his arm. This shield was a defense mechanism to ward off possible wounding. The second anyone would try to address an issue in this brothers' life, he would throw up the shield to protect himself and in the process knock the others down, sometimes even severely wounding them. Then he would lower his shield and ask what they were doing on the ground, having no idea how he could possibly be the cause of the wounding. So this brother would continue to wound people without necessarily even being aware of it. If we are wounding people, let's get healed so it will stop. If we have been wounded by someone, let's forgive the person and let the Holy Spirit bring healing and restoration into our lives. Let's allow the Holy Spirit to deal with our issues, no matter what they are; from pride to self-pity or lack of forgiveness to fear.

When we talk about deep-rooted issues, many of them are mindsets that have developed. If mindsets go unchecked they become strongholds in our lives. The dictionary definition of **stronghold** is *"a place that has been fortified against attack."* The definition of **mindset** is *"a habitual way of thinking."* Ed Silvoso described a stronghold this way, *"A mind-set impregnated with hopelessness that causes us to accept as unchangeable situations that we know are contrary to the will of God."*

The starting point of beginning to address such mindsets is described in 2 Corinthians 10:5 *"...casting down arguments and every high thing that exalts itself against the knowledge of God, bringing every thought into captivity to the obedience of Christ..."* We must begin to address the strongholds in our lives.

Final thought - In this chapter I know that much of what we discussed can be a bit hard to process. It is great to know that the promise of Scripture is that we will walk in the peaceable fruit of righteousness (Hebrews 12:11). Will it be worth it all? Most definitely.

Note: I would like to thank Frank Damazio and Graham Cooke for their teaching and inspiration to me in writing this chapter.

Chapter 4

EFFECTIVE PERSONAL INTERCESSION

I n this time, we are living in, we desperately need effective people of prayer. These are People who refuse to be distracted, sidelined or derailed. Sometimes it can seem as if prayer was designed for a much simpler, quieter time. In our 21st century fast-paced lives, having a daily time of prayer not only seems impractical, but often times seems impossible. Many people today get up in the morning, hit the ground running and don't stop until they fall into bed at night. When we get caught up in this way of living, prayer can seem like just an added burden to an already heavy schedule. Then, if we do manage to fit in some time for prayer, we often get to where we are only praying for our own needs and the things of our own lives. As believers we truly need to come to the place where we can be effective in intercession on a daily basis.

When it comes to times of personal intercession, many of us have a "hit and miss" experience in our times with the Lord. Sometimes our prayer times are simply amazing as we are caught up in God's presence and the flow of His Spirit. Other times it seems like a struggle and we wonder if it is doing any good at all. In my own life, I have had the same experience. I have learned that there are some practical keys to entering into intercession that make it not only effective, but extremely enjoyable. Most of us are not going to continue in something long-term that we do not receive enjoyment from. Let's look at some thoughts and ideas that I call "effectiveness principles" in personal intercession.

Principle #1 - Be Prophetic - Hearing His Voice

When we talk about being prophetic, we are not just talking about the ability to give a prophetic word. One of the meanings of the word **prophesy** is the Hebrew word "Naba" which is *to speak with inspiration*. I found the Webster's dictionary definition of the word **inspiration** to be quite interesting. The first definition refers to breathing; *the act of drawing air into the lungs; the inhaling of air.* As we come into God's presence, we can, in a sense, breathe Him in and be brought into a place of closeness with the Lord where we can you hear His heart.

The next definition sounds as if it came from a Bible commentary, but it is directly from the dictionary; ***The infusion of ideas into the mind by the Holy Spirit****; the conveying into the minds of men ideas, notices or monitions by extraordinary or supernatural influence; or the communication of the divine will to the understanding by suggestions or impressions on the mind, which leave no room to doubt the reality of their supernatural origin.*

So we see that being prophetic really is about inspiration and inspiration is about the Holy Spirit communicating to our hearts and minds that which God would have us know. It is simply getting in touch with God's heart for people and situations. Prophetic insight is not just for "special" people, but for every believer at some level. The key to hearing God's heart is getting in touch with His voice. It is the privilege of every Christ follower to hear the voice of God resounding deep in their heart.

Jesus said in John 10:4, *"When he puts forth his own sheep, he goes before them, and the sheep follow him: **for they know his voice."***

Being prophetic also means tapping into the endless stream of thoughts that God has for us. In Psalm 40:5 we read, *"Many, O LORD my God, are Your wonderful works Which You have done; And **Your thoughts toward us** cannot be recounted to You in order; If I would declare and speak of them, **they are more than can be numbered."*** It is hard to imagine that there are countless number of thoughts that God has for us at any given moment. Not just thoughts, but good thoughts. A big part of intercession is just tapping into that countless number of thoughts, feelings and emotions that God has for people.

Principle #2 - Carry His Burdens

In personal intercession we must learn what it means to carry the burdens God has for each of us individually. The burdens we carry may not be the same as what someone else carries. If we get under a wrong burden, it could get us off-track and blur our focus. Make sure it is the Holy Spirit, the one who places burdens, that is asking you to come under a specific burden. I believe this is one of the primary ways that we become co-laborers and fellow workers with Christ. (1 Corinthians 3:9)

To illustrate this, I would like to tell you the story of a prophetic journey that led me to one of the strongest burdens of intercession I have carried to date. This burden was given to me by the Holy Spirit through a series of dreams and prophetic experiences.

*The Burden for College Students

The first dream: *My friend, Randall Martin, and I were at a university campus. I wasn't sure which university it was at the time, but later realized it was the University of Oregon. We were standing under a breezeway because it was threatening to rain. To our right, and slightly downhill, were about a hundred students gathered in a campus square. They were approximately 50 yards away. Instantly, there came a torrential downpour and a heavy wind. Most of the students ran for cover; however, a group of 20 or 30 raised large umbrellas as if they thought it would be fun to ride out the storm. Suddenly a strong wind picked them up into the air, and many of them dropped to their deaths from 50 or 60 feet. Some were caught up and never came down. As we observed this, we fell on our faces in grief and travail. The next scene was several hours later. The campus was covered with national and international news media. There were many people being interviewed about what they saw happen. It seemed that the nation was being shaken by this event.*

In response to the catastrophe, a major student revival had broken out on the campus and Randall and I were a part of it. We weren't leading the revival; we were just facilitating and watching over it. The students were leading the revival. The students were praying for one another with full-blown signs, wonders, miracles, healings and salvation's happening.

Now we are going to jump forward about three weeks. We were at our home in Glasgow, Scotland when, in the middle of the night, my wife and I were awakened to a noise in our room. It was the sound of the walls and floor and furniture creaking, as if the air in the room was expanding. Soon after, I noticed the music on our laptop had stopped. We have a list of worship songs on iTunes that we play through the night, but it was not playing. I wondered if the power had gone out. A few seconds after I had this thought, the music came back on in the middle of a song from the band Delirious called, **Did You Feel Mountains Tremble**. This song was written in 1994 by Martin Smith and Matt Redman. When the song came back on, this was the verse that was being played:

> *"And here we see that God You're moving*
> *A time of Jubilee is coming*
> *When young and old return to Jesus*
> *Fling wide you heavenly gates*
> *Prepare the way of the risen Lord"*

I heard the Lord speak to my heart, "This is what I want you to hear." It seemed the line "**when young and old return to Jesus**" was being highlighted by the Holy Spirit.

About a week later I had another dream about university aged young people. This one was much more disturbing:

I was at Bob Jones' house in South Carolina. I was standing with he and Bobby Conner, and we were watching a newscast on the television. It was a report on a large group of young people gathering on what seemed to be the top of a high dam, like Hoover Dam in Nevada. It seemed like a spring break party-type atmosphere. Then all of a sudden, I was not watching on television anymore, but I was there. I was standing on a high cliff overlooking the scene. On the left side of the dam there was a chute of water steeply running down. Somebody

71

shouted that they should slide down this chute. The chute was directly beneath where I stood and I could hear the screams as young men and women fell hundreds of feet to their deaths. They had no idea that this chute ended with a straight drop off.

I awoke extremely shaken by what I had seen in the dream. As I spent time in prayer that morning I noted the date, August 30th. I then thought I would look in my journal to see what the date of the first dream was, and it was July 30th. Thirty is the number of the age of maturity in ministry. Jesus, Joseph and David were all 30 years old when they entered the fullness of their calling. I knew that I was on to something.

Then the Lord reminded me about the story of Martin Smith and his near fatal car crash in 1995. This is the Wikipedia account of the crash:

*"On **August 30th** 1995, Martin Smith was driving back from a gig at the Grapevine Festival in Lincolnshire when, in the early hours of the morning and only around the corner from home, he was involved in a serious car accident. (The song "August 30th" on the 'King of Fools' album was written about this event.) The crash turned out to be an important moment in Smith's life and the life of the band."*

I then remembered what happened in our bedroom and the Delirious song. God was beginning to put it all together for me. First, the band **Delirious** was called by God to awaken a generation. The song, **Did You Feel the Mountains Tremble** was just one of their songs God used to speak to a generation of young people, calling them to arise. Then I remembered Bob

Jones talking about the **"Billion Youth Revival"** that is coming. How there is going to be countless millions of young people brought in to the kingdom before the return of Christ.

The primary message of the two dreams was that the enemy wants to bring a pre-emptive strike against this young generation because he sees them as a great threat to the kingdom of darkness. Just as in the life of Moses and Jesus, there was a decree to destroy the deliverer before he reached the age of maturity.

Bob Jones and Bobby Conner are prophets, but they are also fathers in the body of Christ. This generation desperately needs fathers and mothers to pray for them and speak into their lives. The phrase, *"The young and old return to Jesus"* speaks of the multi-generational anointing that God is releasing. And finally, God is about to pour out His Spirit on university campuses around the world.

Most of the day, after the second dream, I was very moved and shaken by what I had experienced. It was all I could do that day to hold back the tears. I was able to share this burden later that evening, August 30th, with the leaders at Glasgow Prophetic Centre. I told them that this was something really on God's heart and asked if we could spend a few minutes in corporate intercession for this generation. The intercession was focused and powerful, many praying with passion for this young adult generation around the world.

*Forward to March 2011

`When I awoke on March 22, 2011, I was thinking about spring break and the experience that I had relating to it the past summer. I went on a prayer hike at a park near our home in Scotland. As I was driving to the park I decided to focus my prayer time on college-age young adults. I prayed for the various spring break gatherings, especially in America. At one point in my walk through the woods, during a time when I was praying that God would defeat the spirit of lawlessness at these events, I had a vision:

*The Spring Break Gathering Vision

In the vision, I was standing on a stage at a spring break concert. I immediately began to pray for those at the event and then I declared a proclamation with force. I took my walking stick and, with both hands raised vertically, hit the stage four or five times. I said, "I declare an end to the spirit of lawlessness and I release the spirit of purity, holiness, integrity and righteousness. Then I felt the leading of the Holy Spirit to preach to this crowd of what I knew to be 3000 young adults. As I began to preach, the place was struck by an earthquake. It was so dramatic that I felt it physically as I was standing on the trail. I had to open my eyes and take a step back to keep from losing my balance. Once I regained my balance, I closed my eyes and immediately reentered the vision. I looked out and saw that the back one third of the outdoor venue was sinking into the earth, along with all the young adults that were in that area. As this happened, the rest of the crowd began to press towards the stage. I saw those hanging over the precipice being pulled up and saved. Once again I began to pray for the crowd that they would have a revelation of Jesus. I ask the Holy Spirit how many remained. He firmly said, "You have 2000 remaining before you,

74

NOW PREACH." I *preached the gospel to them and they **all** responded. I could see angels coming to minister over them as they received salvation. That was the end of the vision.*

After the vision I went back to my car and wrote out what happened in my journal. As I put away the journal, I heard the Spirit say to me "Do you remember what day this is?" Then it hit me. March 22 is my spiritual birthday. On this day, 36 years ago, at the age of 17, I gave my life to Jesus.

Will you join me in continuing to pray for this generation, that the enemy will not prevail in destroying these deliverers before they step into the full maturity of all they are called to; and that God would move powerfully on university campuses all over the world?

Sometimes the burdens that God gives us are ongoing assignments. The burden for young adults is like that for me. Other times the burdens are for a shorter time and season, but they are still important. We must come to the place where we can receive, carry and steward the burdens the Lord gives us.

Principle #3 - Take Joy Very Seriously

As we carry burdens in intercession, it must be from a foundation of joy in our lives. It is vitally important that we maintain a lifestyle of joy and not let the burden bearing, and sometimes heavy and hard struggles in prayer, cause us to be heavy, overly serious, negative and critical. Nehemiah 8:10 says *"for the joy of the LORD is your strength"* and we will need that strength in intercession. There is a strong connection between joy and praise, so let your intercession times always include times of praise. (Psalm 100:4)

A foundational verse on joy is this. *"The ransomed of the LORD shall return, and come to Zion with singing, with ever-lasting **joy** on their heads. They shall obtain **joy and gladness**, and **sorrow and sighing shall flee away.**"* (Isaiah 35:10) It seems in general that there is an increased amount of reasons to be downcast, disheartened, discouraged and depressed. I believe more than ever we are going to need the joy that is talked about in this verse. This joy and gladness is not only to strengthen us, but it is given by the Lord to counteract and destroy sorrow and sighing. The sadness has been in response to many hard things, but now the Lord is bringing a flood of joy that is directly related to the release of His presence. (Psalm 16:11) This joy is available to us so that we begin to live from the inside. We need to let the joy of heaven within us completely overwhelm and defuse the negative and hard pressures that surround us.

When Corrie Ten Boom was asked how she dealt with the horrors of the Nazi concentration camp that she and her family were in, she responded simply, **"Joy runs deeper than despair."** We need to see joy as, not just a supernatural remedy for the hard things we face, but as part of our divine inheritance as believers. The thing about joy is that it is not connected directly to circumstances. Unlike happiness that is connected to a happening, joy is something else altogether. It is a heavenly spiritual gift, as well as a fruit of the Spirit. The word happy is mentioned six times in the New Testament, but the word joy is mentioned 60 times; ten times as much. I think the emphasis of

Scripture is on joy. Here on earth, we were never designed to handle life's low points within our own strength. We are designed to be receivers of God's joy in tough times in order to receive the strength to see us through.

This is something that God is very passionate about. **You might say that God is very serious about joy and gladness.** He is so serious that He is not offering this to us as an **option,** but **a mandate**. This serious tone is reflected in Deuteronomy 28:47-48. *"Because you did not serve the LORD your God with joy and gladness of heart, for the abundance of everything, therefore you shall serve your enemies..."* The rest of these verses give a strong indication that our refusing to serve the Lord with joy will open the door for unbelief that leads to a poverty spirit operating in our lives. Some would say, "But those are Old Testament verses." Then how about New Testament ones like, "**Rejoice** in the Lord always. Again I will say, **rejoice**!" (Philippians 4:4). Or "For the kingdom of God is not eating and drinking, but righteousness and peace and **joy** in the Holy Spirit." (Romans 14:17) CS Lewis said, **"Joy is the serious business of heaven."**

Our Father in heaven loves us immensely and does not want us to live in a continual state of sadness, negativity, unbelief and a critical spirit. We were created for so much more than this. **I also believe that serving with the absence of joy cripples us in our effectiveness to minister to and reach others.** What drew me to Christ was the fact that I was around believers with genuine joy that caused me to know that they had something I did not have. What is it that people see when they look at us? Do they see the negativity or do they see joy? We must rise up again and return to the joy of the Lord. I remember about a five-year season in my life that I lived devoid of the joy of the Lord. It wasn't something that happened overnight, but gradually joy left my life. I then heard a message about the **Joy of the Lord** and it hit me. I repented and asked God to refill me with His joy and determined that from that day I would not lose it again. **We must choose joy.**

When we talk about choosing joy, does that mean that we will never experience grieving, sorrow, disappointment and discouragement again? No, not likely. Does it mean that we are in some kind of denial to reality and are not facing things truthfully? Not if we have real joy. **It does mean that the life of God living inside of us will bring a joy that will carry us through.** David said in Psalm 23:4 *"Yea, though I walk through the valley of the shadow of death, I will fear no evil; for You are with me."* God doesn't always remove us from the circumstances, but He promises His presence, manifested through joy, will see us through.

Some may say, "Yeah but you don't know what I'm going through or what I'm facing. It is not going to be fixed by just deciding to choose joy." Yes, but it could be a starting point to begin to align yourself with God and believe that He is good. So today why don't we take the first step and **choose joy**.

Principle #4 - Guard Your Sensitivity

As people of prayer, we are wired by God to be sensitive. Therefore, we are easily moved spiritually and emotionally, and sometimes even physically. We must guard our sensitivity because we have a tendency to be easily offended, hurt and overwhelmed by people and situations. We must learn to be strengthened inwardly and let the Lord shore us up in these areas. We must learn to cast our cares upon Him because he cares for us. (1 Peter 5:7)

*The Forgiveness Factor

This brings us to an area of obedience to God's Word that will bring much freedom, release, victory and breakthrough, not only in our intercession but our lives as well. However, if we do not attend to this area, we will be opening ourselves to bondage, defeat, frustration and stagnation. The area I am referring to is forgiveness. Dealing with offenses and hurts is vital to our unhindered flow in intercession. Lack of forgiveness builds a wall across our path and stops us cold in our effectiveness.

Firstly, we need to deal with that which brings a rift between us and our brothers and sisters in Christ. Jesus said, *"Therefore if you bring your gift to the altar, and there remember that your brother has something against you, leave your gift there before the altar, and go your way. First be reconciled to your brother, and then come and offer your gift."* (Matthew 5:23, 24) Then also, we must forgive those who don't know the Lord who have offended us.

One of the things we need to get past before we can forgive is the idea that if I forgive someone, especially someone who has purposefully and maliciously hurt me, then they will be getting away with it. We must understand that in the long run, nobody gets away with anything. The heavenly security cameras are running 24/7 and ultimately every person will stand before God and give account. Paul said it this way, *"But why do you judge your brother? Or why do you show contempt for your brother? For we shall all stand before the judgment seat of Christ."* (Romans 14:10) Our job is to not worry so much about others, but to allow the Holy Spirit to pinpoint any instances where we haven't forgiven.

A few years ago I was spending some time praying about some provision for our ministry. I was asking the Lord about a dream that I had. In the dream I was talking to a person that previously had offended me. While I was talking to them another person walked up to me and handed me a $5,000 check. During the prayer time, I was asking God about the check I had seen in the dream. I was surprised at what He said to me. He said, "I'm not going to release that provision until you get it right with that person." Now this left me a bit frustrated. I thought I had work through forgiveness. I talked to the person, sent e-mails, prayed out forgiveness and tried to not speak against them.

One of the ways we can tell that we are not quite there and still working through forgiveness is that, when a certain person's name is mentioned, we have a negative reaction. We find ourselves being tempted to say, "Well let me tell you about so and so." I had remembered just such a time when this person's name was mentioned and I had a reaction. So I agreed with the Lord that I had not completely forgiven this person. I said, "Okay, what should I do? How can I work through forgiveness with this person?" He replied, "What did I tell you to do with your enemies?" I then remembered Matthew 5:43-45. Jesus said, *"You have heard that it was said, 'You shall love your neighbor and hate your enemy.' But I say to you, **love** your enemies, **bless** those who* *curse you,* **do good** *to those who hate you, and* **pray for** *those who spitefully use you and persecute you, that you may be sons of your Father in heaven."* In these verses there are four positives: **loving, blessing, doing good and praying for**. These are to be our positive responses to the four negatives that are coming against us by our human enemies: **hatred, cursing, spitefully using and persecuting.** If this is the standard for how we treat our enemies, how much higher is the standard for how we should treat our brothers and sisters in Christ?

I then surrendered and asked the Lord if there was anything specifically I should do in light of these verses. I felt the Lord prompt me to send the person a Facebook message (yes God does use Facebook) that had all four of those positives included in it. So I wrote a message in such a way that a person wouldn't recognize that it was from Matthew 5. I felt like the Lord was pleased. When it comes to areas of offence, if we are quick to forgive, we will find it harder to be offended the next time.

Principle #5 - Be Consistent

To grow in personal intercession, consistent daily time with the Lord is very important. It is always good to commit to a longer time daily than you think you can handle. There is a friend of mine who had made a commitment to daily prayer. He told me of a time where the Lord had been testing him. For a period of 30 days he went to prayer each morning with no sense of the presence of God. He decided that, no matter what, he would continue to pray each day. Towards the end of the 30 day's it became a struggle but he continued. Then on the 31st day, as he walked into his study, he was overwhelmed by the glory of the

Lord. For the next 30 days God met him in a powerful way each day. His consistency paid off.

It is easy to be consistent in something if you love what you are doing. Once again, it is not about performing, achieving or adopting a religious duty. It is about wanting to spend time with Him. If we got a message from a famous person that we admired telling us that they wanted to spend some time with us, we would be excited, thrilled and overjoyed. We would be telling all of our friends about the great opportunity we had. Then if that person told us that they wanted to meet with us on a regular basis, we wouldn't be overwhelmed. How much greater is the invitation we have received to spend time daily with the king of the universe, the one whom no man can be compared to.

Principle #6 Operate from a Basis of Rest

As people of prayer, one of the most valuable lessons we can learn is the truth of receiving and walking in the rest of God. The rest of God, as well as the peace of God, allows us to deal with the tremendous external pressures of life and not be overcome by them. One of the lessons that science teaches us is that there is 15 pounds per square inch of pressure on the human body at all times. The reason that we do not feel this pressure is that there is an equal amount of outward pressure coming from within our bodies simultaneously. The rest of God and the peace of God is that which gives us the inner strength to deal with whatever outward pressures we face in life.

Chapters 3 and 4 of Hebrews speak to us about entering into

God's rest. One of the most important things to be learned from these chapters is the principle of hearing God's voice and heeding it. It says three times in these two chapters, *"Today, if you will hear his voice, do not harden your hearts."* Having a heart relationship with God is key to receiving His rest. These chapters also speak of several things that will be roadblocks for us to entering the rest. The first is **testing God** by trying to see how much can be gotten away with. *"Where your fathers tested Me, tried Me, and saw My works forty years."* (Hebrews 3:9) The next is **unbelief** by not taking Him at His word. *"Beware, brethren, lest there be in any of you an evil heart of unbelief in departing from the living God."* (Hebrews 3:12) *And* there is **deceitfulness of sin** or being deceived into thinking sin is okay. *"But exhort one another daily, while it is called* **TODAY**, *lest any of you be hardened through the deceitfulness of sin."* (Hebrews 3:13) Then finally we have **disobedience to His voice** by refusing to do what He says. *"And to whom did He swear that they would not enter His rest, but to those who did not obey?"* (Hebrews 3:18)

On the other hand, there are pro-active actions we can take to enter the **rest of God**. The first is to **cease from your own works** by not living life in your own strength. *"For he who has entered His rest has himself also ceased from his works as God did from His."* (Hebrews 4:10) *The* next is **holding fast to your relationship with God.** *"For we have become partakers of Christ if we hold the beginning of our confidence steadfast to the end."* (Hebrews 3:14) Then you should **let the Word of God work deeply in your life.** *"For the Word of God is living and powerful, and sharper than any two-edged sword, piercing even to the division of soul and spirit, and of joints and marrow, and is a discerner of the thoughts and intents of* the heart." (Hebrews 4:12) Finally, you should let God give you grace for all that you need. *"For we do not have a High Priest who cannot sympathize with our weaknesses, but was in all points tempted as we are, yet without sin. Let us therefore come boldly to the throne of grace that we may obtain mercy and find grace to help in time of need."* (Hebrews 4:15)

As we surrender completely to Jesus, we can be assured that no matter what happens we can trust the rest and peace of God, which will not only see us through but will allow tremendous victories to be won. Even when intercession and warfare can get intense, we still need to operate from a place of being established and grounded in the rest of God.

Principle #7 - Maintain a Lifestyle of Faith

To illustrate the idea of a lifestyle of faith, I have included an article that my wife, Darla, wrote for one of our newsletters during the time we were living in Scotland:

*Living IN Faith by Darla Bachelder

I have been going back and forth with the Lord about writing this article for several days now... "But I am not a writer, Lord. Mike is the writer. Can't you just ask him to write it?" *"But I am speaking to you. This is a story for you to tell."* "Please, Lord, not me!!!!" ... and so on and so forth. After two hours of trying to ignore the Lord while lying in bed early this morning, I finally gave in. This story is mine to tell.

In September of 2006, after reading the book "Reece Howells Intercessor" the Lord led Mike to lay down his successful painting business and give his life to full-time ministry, with a focus on intercession. Mike agreed with the Lord that He would step out of a wage earning job and the Lord agreed that he would be our keeper and provider for the rest of our days. (Psalm 121) You can probably imagine that when Mike came home that morning from one of his many prayer hikes and told me this story, I was at first shocked and even doubtful. Mike was ever the provider. While raising five kids, he worked harder than any man I have ever known in order to ensure we all had a good life. If extra money was needed for something, he just picked up an extra house to paint and worked on the weekends and evenings to bring in what was needed. How would we make it with that option removed? Yet, as Mike shared with me the story of his encounter with the Lord, I knew without a doubt that it was truly God calling us into a lifestyle of faith and complete dependency on Him.

It has been an interesting journey as we have endeavored to **live by faith**. I continued in my position as an office administrator for our church until the Lord released us as missionaries in September of 2008. So even in those first two years of transition, we had a bit of a cushion with my income, as well as a small monthly gift that Mike received from the church. But since heading for Scotland in 2008, we have solely been living by the provision of God, through gifts from those who have been prompted by His spirit to support us, or by random financial blessings from random sources. There are a few gifts that have been steady and we can generally count on receiving each month, but most of the time we never really know how the provision will be manifested. It has been challenging at time, but mostly exciting to watch and see how the Lord will provide.

I was thinking about the idea of **living BY faith** one day and I felt the Lord challenge me to begin to **live IN faith**. There is a definite difference! I have been living BY faith for many years... stirring up faith when necessary to believe God to provide for a need. And He has always been faithful. But I am now also learning to live IN faith... in a state of constant knowing that, *"my God will supply all my need according to His riches in glory by Christ Jesus"* (Philippians 4:19) and *"He is able to do exceedingly, abundantly above all that we ask or think."* (Ephesians 3:20) It is a daily knowing that we will have what we need. When the food supply gets low and we use the last of the milk or eggs or bread, I can have confidence that before we need it again, the Lord will supply it... and He does. When we were in need of a car for the ministry here in Scotland, the Lord made amazing provision for us. The other day, just after Mike and I prayed together for a need that we were aware of, I turned on the computer and immediately saw a PayPal contribution come in through someone that the Lord had prompted to give. As we are away from our children, we have faith that God loves our kids and grandkids even more than we do, and He will take care of them for us... and He does!

Now, not everyone is called to leave their jobs for the sake of ministry. God's provision comes in so many ways. Some are blessed with amazing jobs or businesses that God has provided, and are able to use their resources to help further the kingdom by giving and sowing into ministries. **We are so blessed by**

people who have committed to support us as we continue this journey.

Mike says, *"The Lord wants to meet us, not necessarily at the point of our need, but at the point of our faith."* This is why I am choosing not to just **live BY faith**, but to also **live IN faith**. It is a lot easier to trust Him constantly to meet our needs, not just work up the faith as needed. *"Now faith is the substance of things hoped for, the evidence of things not seen."* (Hebrews. 11:1) *I* **believe it is by living IN faith that the things we hope for and the things we cannot see become our manifested provision.**

So there... I've been obedient and shared from my heart. I'm still arguing with the Lord a bit about this one... **but in the end, I know He wins!**

Principle #8 - Get in a Flow with the Holy Spirit

In prayer, as you get into a flow of the Holy Spirit, it will be as if time loses its effect. Literally hours can seem like minutes. To get in the flow, I find it helpful to get my body into it. I usually walk, move my arms and even act out what I am praying about. As you start, the Holy Spirit will take over and you will find yourself flowing in intercession. Another helpful thing to do is to take the Scriptures and turn them into prayers. There is always an anointing on the Word when it is prayed out.

In Romans 8:26-27, the Holy Spirit is known as the "Spirit of intercession." The enablement for intercession only comes from Him. Jesus said in John 7:38, *"He who believes in Me, as the Scripture has said, out of his heart will flow rivers of living water."*

The word for "heart" in this verse is **Koilia** which means "abdomen" or "matrix." A matrix is: *the place where anything is formed or produced.*

Intercession should never be about striving and struggling in the flesh. It's about letting the river flow and allowing ourselves to be carried on that river. Mental focus and determination is not the source of this flow. It is by the Holy Spirit, as He draws us into effortless prayers, in that the words we are actually praying originate in our spirit and not in our mind. If you tend towards an intellectual, analytical approach, this could be a struggle for you. Ask the Holy Spirit for the grace to be primarily Spirit led and motivated, allowing your mind to follow.

A very effective means by which the Holy Spirit can bring us into a flow is by praying in the Spirit. One of the things I am most thankful for in my life is the tremendous honor and privilege of receiving the baptism of the Holy Spirit. As we pray in our prayer language our spirit is built up, strengthened and tuned in to the Holy Spirit. I find it helpful to start my intercession time praying in the Spirit. It allows me to step into the flow for that time.

Another aspect of flowing in the Holy Spirit during our prayer time is incorporating worship music. You may want to pick something to play in the background, but make sure that the words in the music are not going to be a distraction to you. There are times that you will want to just worship, but when you move into intercession, let the music support the prayer.

Principle #9 - Pray with Passion

When we talk about praying with passion, we are not just referring to volume or even someone with a loud, boisterous personality. We are talking about praying with the passion and compassion of Jesus. In James 5:16 we read that, *"the effectual fervent prayer of a righteous man avails much."* The words "effectual fervent" are from the Greek word **energeo** which means "to be mighty in". (Strong's) The words "avails much" carries the idea of "making much power available." This is how the Amplified Bible says it:

"Confess to one another therefore your faults (your slips, your false steps, your offenses, your sins) and pray [also] for one another, that you may be healed and restored [to a spiritual tone of mind and heart]. The earnest (heartfelt, continued) prayer of a righteous man makes tremendous power available [dynamic in its working]."

As we pray fervently, with passion, the power of the Holy Spirit is released. In other types of prayer, it is perfectly fine to pray in subdued tones. But in intercession, there must be passion. It is possible to pray passionately and quietly at the same time. It is not volume, but intensity, that makes the difference. In Jeremiah 29:12-13, having your heart in it seems to count. *"Then you will call upon Me and go and pray to Me, and I will listen to you. And you will seek Me and find Me, when you search for Me with all your heart."*

Final Thought - As we grasp the importance and value of intercession, we will be positioning ourselves to step into cooperation with the Holy Spirit to bring God's will into a living reality. One of the most important things we can learn about personal intercession is that you actually learn more by doing it than you do by just learning about it. We are all in the school of the Holy Spirit in our daily times with the Lord. As we are faithful and consistent, we will build a life of prayer that truly will be effective and make a difference.

Chapter 5

INTERCESSION AND THE BURNING HEART

I ntercession requires that we allow God to give us a burning heart of passion for Him and that which is on His heart. The Lord first brought this idea of a burning heart home to me was when I was with a group of people having lunch with Bob Jones. Someone asked Bob if he saw anything from the Lord for me, and Bob made this statement, "The next thing for you is the burning heart." I instantly knew that it was something that I needed to look into. The primary verse in scripture that refers to this is Luke 24:32, *"And they said one to another, 'Did not our heart burn within us, while he talked with us by the way, and while he opened to us the scriptures?'"*

The disciples on the road to Emmaus, once they realized it was Jesus they had been with, knew that something had happened. Their hearts were on fire with passion because of being with Him. It is the "being with Him" that makes all the difference. You will not last long in intercession without receiving a burning heart of passion from the Lord. We need to become people on fire. John Wesley said it this way, *"Catch on fire with enthusiasm and people will come for miles to watch you burn."*

Jesus demonstrated the burning heart while He was on earth. It was said of Him in John 2:17, *"Then his disciples remembered that it is written, "The zeal of your house will consume me."* His heart burned in prayer, in weeping, in the garden and on the cross. Today His heart still burns for continents, nations, peoples and individuals. Each of us is the object of God's burning heart of love as is stated in Ephesians 2:4, *"But God, who is rich in mercy, for his great love wherewith he loved us."*

Developing a Burning Heart

Jesus answered him, "The first of all the commandments is: 'Hear, O Israel, the LORD our God, the LORD is one. And you shall love the LORD your God with all your heart, with all your soul, with all your mind, and with all your strength.' This is the first commandment." Mark 12:29-30

As we come into relationship with Jesus, He gives us a burning heart of love for Him and His kingdom. It is the divine enablement to keep the first commandment first.

It is His job to impart that flame to us, and it is our job to tend the flame and keep it burning. Many of us can think of someone we knew that was on fire for God at one time. Then it seemed, as time passed, something happened and their fire waned, and for some, their fire even went out. In my early years as a believer I had the great privilege of being friends with a man who was, at that point, one of the most on-fire believers I had met. He had an amazing relationship with God. He was all about prayer, worship, Bible reading, and evangelism. I fell out of touch with this young man for several years. When I saw him again, I didn't know what had happened during that time, but he was no longer the on-fire believer that I knew before. It seemed that the affairs and daily tribulations of life had quenched his fire for the Lord that once burned bright. Jesus referred to it as losing your first love.

"Nevertheless I have this against you, that you have left your first love. Remember therefore from where you have fallen; repent and do the first works, or else I will come to you quickly and remove your lampstand from its place --- unless you repent." Revelations 2:5-6

Michael W. Smith has a song called "I Miss the Way" that describes this kind of person:

Once a true believer
Once there was a fire in your soul
You were the epitome of blessed faith astir
With thirst for holiness
And hunger for the Word

Now you move in other circles
To the beat of different drums
And I see only glimpses of the one you used to be
The inspiration that you were to me

Chorus:
I miss the way His love would dance within your eyes
I miss the way His heart was the soul of your life
And somewhere in the saddest part of heaven's room
Our Father sheds a tear for you
He's missing you, too

We must realize that if we are to have burning hearts for Jesus, the enemy is going to do whatever he can to put that flame out. That flame makes you dangerous in the eyes of the enemy. He will try to bring everything, from the cares and affairs of life (2

Timothy 2:4) to the enticements of the flesh and the world. (1 John 2:16)

The passionate flame of love for Jesus is described in Song of Solomon 8:6-7. *"Set me as a seal upon your heart, as a seal upon your arm; for love is as strong as death, Jealousy as cruel as the grave; its **flames are flames of fire, a most vehement flame**. Many waters cannot quench love, nor can the floods drown it. If a man would give for love all the wealth of his house, it would be utterly despised."*

Here are some practical steps we can do, that will help us not only maintain the burning heart we have, but see that flame increase.

Utmost Obedience by Profound Faith

In the western world I think we struggle with the idea that we do not belong to ourselves. Do I really believe that *I am not my own for I was bought at a price*? (1 Corinthians 6:19-20) When I call Him "Lord" do I really mean it? A big part of taking up the cross daily and following Him is giving Him the reins of my life and allowing Him the place to direct my life in any way He chooses. We need to have radical obedience that is not optional, occasional or convenience-based. The reason many people don't ask God about His will for their lives is that they are afraid of what the answer might be, especially when it relates to personal sacrifice. We must come to a place where we are willing to do anything and go anywhere. It's okay to admit if you are not there yet, as long as you are willing to allow God to lead you in that direction.

Back in 1999 God began to speak to Darla and I about moving from Oregon to North Carolina. As we were in the process of determining God's will, He was very kind and gracious to give us numerous confirmations. We started seeing things to do with North Carolina almost on a daily basis. I had two dreams about cities in North Carolina that I didn't know existed.

One of the most dramatic confirmations happened one day as I was looking at a USA atlas. On the North Carolina page, I noticed some statistics listed on the top right corner. I found out that North Carolina is the 10th largest state in population and the 29th largest in land mass. Then I looked over to the Oregon page and found out that Oregon is the 10th largest state in land mass and 29th largest in population. I couldn't get those numbers out of my head. When I ask the Lord about it I sensed that He wanted me to look up 10:29 verses.

I started with the Old Testament and found nothing that seemed to fit. Then I came to Mark 10:29 and was stunned when I read what I consider to be one of most powerful sending verses in the Bible. Jesus said:

"Assuredly, I say to you, there is no one who has left house or brothers or sisters or father or mother or wife or children or lands, for My sake and the gospel's, who shall not receive a hundredfold now in this time houses and brothers and sisters and mothers and children and lands, with persecutions and in the age to come, eternal life."

Even with all the confirmation and faith that the Lord was leading us forward in this, it was still one of the hardest decisions we've ever had to make in our lives. In Oregon, we lived within 20 miles of where I was born and Darla was raised. We were surrounded by loving family and wonderful life-long friends. We were on the leadership team at the church we attended and Darla was a staff secretary there. We did not know a single person in the town the Lord was directing us to in North Carolina. We had a family meeting with our children and spent time talking and praying. Together as a family, we agreed to walk forward into this new adventure, realizing there was really no other choice for us. Our daughter, Amy, 13 years old at the time, said it best for all of us, "I know it's what the Lord is asking us to do, and it's the right thing for us to do, but I'm going to cry a million tears doing it." And we all did. But it led us into a life of adventures none of us will ever regret. Many times, utmost obedience does require great sacrifice, but the benefits of being obedient far outweigh the sacrifices.

In our obedience, we do not know all the reasons why God is asking something of us. We had a strong sense that our move to North Carolina had as much to do with our children as it did with us. They were between the ages of 10 and 16 at the time and we knew that this would affect various things in their lives, everything from their God-calling to practical things like who they would marry and where they would settle. It was also our move to North Carolina that eventually opened the doors for us to be involved in ministry in the nation of Scotland.

We must trust God in our obedience to Him. To obey the Lord isn't always easy, but it is always good and it is always worth it. The ability to walk in utmost obedience comes as we increase in profound faith. The 16 individuals named in Hebrews 11 understood this.

I have often thought about what it would be like to be in a position to be martyred for the Lord. Talk about a burning heart, the martyrs that I have read about had it. The burning heart will not only cause you to go where He asks you to go and do what He asks you to do, it will also require that you say what He asks you to say. I noticed something that every martyr has in common. The reason they became martyrs in the first place is that they simply refused to keep silent. So how does this relate to intercession? As we step into the place of obedience in intercession we will open our mouths and pray no matter what it costs us. God will release profound faith to us to believe Him for even the impossible.

Draw From the Flames of Others

It is obvious that we are shaped and influenced by the people that we are close to. It is no different in developing a heart of passion for the Lord. This is why the disciples were together in one accord in the upper room. Their unity positioned them to receive the fire of the Holy Spirit. Logs on a fire burn much brighter together than apart. Find someone who loves God passionately and draw from their flame. It is also helpful to be around people that will encourage you in your passionate pursuit of God, rather than those who try to squelch or put out your flame. It seems there is no shortage of people who will be quick to tell you what you shouldn't do or can't be. Often, as these people attempt to speak into your life, they really think they are helping you. It could be a family member or friend who doesn't quite get what you're all about. Your passion for God doesn't seem to make sense to them.

Then there are the religious folks who not only don't understand you, but will be offended and put off by you and your "extreme" devotion. Jesus dealt with the same crowd, known as Pharisees. The Pharisees come from an ancient tribe called the "Youcants" (not really). They were always telling Jesus, "**You can't** do this and **you can't** do that." One tactic that the enemy uses the most to douse the flames in our hearts is well-intended people. Many times these people are thinking they are helping us, but in actuality they have become "wet blankets" upon the flame that is burning in our hearts. We must learn to become guardians and tenders of our own flame. The best way to deal with these types of people is to graciously agree to disagree and then shake off the heavy religious condemnation, forgive and continue to walk on in your fire for God.

We need to find those in our lives that can blow on our flame by encouraging us, praying for us and, yes, sometimes speaking the truth in love to us. This is why it is good to seek out fathers and mothers in the faith that will encourage us to burn even brighter.

Another way to draw from the flames of others is by reading or hearing the stories of people who have lived a life on fire for God. The first place to start is the Bible. Our first source of inspiration is the life of Jesus. As we read and study His life, only then will His passion be imparted to us. Then there are the other great ones in Scripture like the apostle Paul, the disciples and the heroes of Hebrews 11. In church history there are many great heroes of the faith, past and present, which we can draw inspiration from. Some of my heroes are Rees Howells, David Livingstone, Smith Wigglesworth, CS Lewis and Jim Elliot. There are many who are alive today that are also an inspiration. We need to receive ministry from those whom God has set as flaming fires.

In Psalm 104:4 these flaming ones are referred to, *"Who makes His angels spirits, His **ministers a flame of fire**."* The Hebrew word for ministers is "sharath" which means *"to attend to as a worshiper."* The Hebrew word for flame is "lahat" which means ***"to blaze, burnt up, set on fire, flaming, kindle."*** The word fire is "aysh" means *"burning, fiery, fire, flaming, hot."* The idea is that those who are attending to God in worship, by ministering to Him, are typically the ones whom He will make a flaming fire. In your search for those you can draw from, look for someone who is a consistent, passionate worshiper of God. These are the people you need to draw inspiration from.

There are times when God will arrange for us to meet someone who will stoke the fire of God in us. In my early 20s I had just such an encounter. I was with a group from Oregon on a short-term mission trip to the UK. On one of our days off we had the great privilege of exploring the city of York. We noticed that in 1980, there was not much of what you would call "Christian" in the nation at that time. No Christian TV, no Christian radio, and no Christian bookstores that we could see. So as my friend, Scott Hammond, and I were walking down a narrow cobblestone street, we noticed a small shop with cards in the window with Scriptures on them.

We decided to check out the shop. There was an elderly woman behind the counter, so I went up to her and asked about the cards in the front. She asked us if we were Christians and I told her that we were. Have you ever met someone whom you quickly realize is longing for fellowship? Well it was apparent that this woman was very glad to see us. She asked what we were doing and we told her we were on a short-term mission trip. Then she began to share with us about her deep relationship with God and we found ourselves in awe. She made one statement that penetrated deep into my heart and I have never forgotten it. She said, *"I have been walking with Jesus for 60 years, and if I had a thousand lives to give I would give every one of them to Jesus Christ."*

By the expression of glory on her face you could tell she meant it. It was like she was saying she wouldn't keep ten, five or even one for herself. Her words settled deep into my heart. So much so that every time I share this story I can't help the tears that come to my eyes. I was so impacted by her testimony. I left that shop with an increased determination to live all out for Jesus the rest of my days, and to let my heart burn for Him. Each one of us only has one life to give. Let's begin by giving our life in passionate prayer to Him.

Seek and Destroy Lukewarmness

The idea of becoming lukewarm is from Revelation 3:14-16. *"And to the angel of the church of the Laodiceans write, 'These things says the Amen, the Faithful and True Witness, the Beginning of the creation of God: 'I know your works, that you are neither cold nor hot. I could wish you were cold or hot. So then, because you are lukewarm, and neither cold nor hot, I will vomit you out of My mouth.'"* The tone of the Master's voice here is not anger or condemnation, it is passion. For Him to make the statement that He would rather have us cold than lukewarm is astonishing. Lukewarmness is subtly deceptive. We can begin to cool off almost without being aware of it. We need to be intentional guardians of our own flame. We must go after anything that would cause us to drift from our simple devotion to Christ. (2 Corinthians 11:3) In Proverbs 4:23 we are told to, *"Keep your heart with all diligence, for out of it spring the issues of life."*

If we find ourselves cooling off in our passion for Jesus, there are some negative ramifications that will result. The first thing is that it will affect the quality and quantity of our prayer life. Prayer just won't seem that important. Worship and time in the Word will be affected also. The next thing is that as we slip into lukewarmness. The things of the world will begin to look more attractive to us. When we walk with a burning heart we will see the world for what it really is, and we will also see the proper relationship to it. Lukewarmness also will open the door to all kinds of negative emotions and attitudes. Criticism, negativity and a downcast heart could develop. Our burning heart is going to be that which keeps us in close relationship with God, not loving the world, and being full of the joy of the Lord.

Lukewarmness will also cause us to slip into what I call "maintenance mode" Christianity. We will find ourselves not living with purpose and destiny, but with a "just getting by until Jesus comes" attitude. We need to understand that living wholeheartedly for Him is the only way to live. There isn't anything else out there that compares. Those who live with a burning heart will someday enter glory and be so glad that they chose Him, and chose to live as passionate pursuers of God. Those believers who settle for less will be regretfully wishing they had chosen the surrendered life. Jim Elliot said it this way, *"He is no fool who gives what he cannot keep to gain what he cannot lose."*

In developing a burning heart, our goal should be to have a consistent and increasing fire that will last, not only years and decades, but to the end of our days. When our torch is lit for Jesus, we need to strive for a consistent flame. It's like the flame that is lit at the beginning of the Olympic Games. There are preparations made to ensure that the flame will burn consistently until the end of the games. We need to settle it in our hearts now that, no matter what, our flame for Him will remain consistent and even increase, and will never go out.

Having a consistent flame doesn't mean that there are not hard things we will go through. What it means is that, no matter what we go through, we should never come to the place where we turn our back on the Lord and let our flame go out. No matter what happens, we need to remember He is good and He is worthy of our devotion to the end.

Bill Johnson said this in referring to hard and difficult things we go through: *"Trust in the Lord with all of your heart, it actually has to mean something. It is not a challenge when everything is going well. There is faith that brings answers, and there is enduring faith that brings answers, and then there is Romans 8:28. ('And we know that all things work together for good to those who love God, to those who are the called according to His purpose.') Do you understand that that promise, Romans 8:28, isn't even necessary if there aren't some things that make it past faith and make it past enduring faith?* (From the message The Dual Purpose of Power)

One of the things we must understand is that **a burning heart is forged in the fires of brokenness.** Suffering, disappointment, heart ache and betrayal are part of this life. In it all, we should have the attitude of Paul when he said in Romans 8:18. *"For I consider that the sufferings of this present time are not worthy to be compared with the glory which shall be revealed in us."* Also in Romans 8:35-37, *"Who shall separate us from the love of Christ? Shall tribulation, or distress, or persecution, or famine, or nakedness, or peril, or sword? As it is written:*

> *"For Your sake we are killed all day long; We are accounted as sheep for the slaughter.' Yet in all these things we are more than conquerors through Him who loved us."*

Tend Your Own Fire

Ultimately we are responsible to tend and care for our own flame. No matter what happens, we cannot blame God, others or the enemy for the state of our love, passion and pursuit of God. It is not only our intensity of pursuit that is important, but the purity and quality of it. We are to make sure that our pursuit remains pure. We need to guard our fire from being polluted with such things as spiritual pride, selfish ambition, extreme supernatural experiences and false doctrine (teaching). Pure zeal is always teachable, humble, meek, kind, submissive and loving. Everything we do as a result of a burning heart should be grounded in the Word of God. If it does not look like the characteristics and traits given to us in scripture, we are risking a contaminated fire.

Strange Fire or Pure Devotion

In the book of Leviticus there is a true story that speaks of the necessity of a pure fire. *"And Nadab and Abihu, the sons of Aaron, took either of them his censer and put fire therein, and put incense thereon, and **offered strange fire** before the LORD, which he commanded them not. And there went out fire from the LORD, and devoured them, and they died before the LORD."* (Leviticus 10:1-2)

Paul talks about the importance of maintaining a pure devotion to Christ, and how the enemy might try to get in. *"But [now] I am fearful, lest that even as the serpent beguiled Eve by his cunning, so your minds may be corrupted and seduced from wholehearted and sincere and **pure devotion** to Christ."* (2 Corinthians 11:3, AMP)

The enemy will try to get us to go too far, or back off and step into religious duty, orphan mindset living and lukewarmness. In maintaining a burning heart, let's endeavor to keep our fire, our passion and our devotion as pure as possible.

Burn with a Love for the Truth

Another way to maintain a pure flame is to be a lover of the truth; the truth of whom God is, the truth of scripture, and the truth of sound doctrine. Don't let the word "doctrine" scare you. It simply means "teaching". The enemy would love to get us off course, believing in something that would contaminate our flame. We need to remain on a solid foundation, which is having a life based on the Word of God. One of the great dangers that we face today is the whole area of false teachings and false teachers. We need to have great discernment as we approach the return of the Lord. This is how Paul, Peter and Jude put it:

"But know this, that in the last days' perilous times will come: For men will be lovers of themselves, lovers of money, boasters, proud, blasphemers, disobedient to parents, unthankful, unholy, unloving, unforgiving, slanderers, without self-control, brutal, despisers of good, traitors, headstrong, haughty, lovers of pleasure rather than lovers of God, having a form of godliness but denying its power. And from such people turn away! For of this sort are those who creep into households and make captives of gullible women loaded down with sins, led away by various lusts, always learning and never able to come to the knowledge of the truth." (2 Timothy 3:1-7)

"You're going to find that there will be times when people will have no **stomach for solid teaching***, but will fill up on* **spiritual junk food**—*catchy opinions that tickle their fancy. They'll turn their backs on truth and chase mirages. But you—keep your eye on what you're doing; accept the hard times along with the good; keep the Message alive; do a thorough job as God's servant."* (2 Timothy 4:3-5 The Message)

"But there were also false prophets among the people, even as there will be **false teachers** *among you, who will secretly bring in destructive heresies, even denying the Lord who bought them, and bring on themselves swift destruction. And many will follow their destructive ways, because of whom the way of truth will be*

blasphemed. By covetousness they will exploit you with deceptive words; for a long time, their judgment has not been idle, and their destruction does not slumber." (2 Peter 2:1-3)

"Beloved, while I was very diligent to write to you concerning our common salvation, I found it necessary to write to you exhorting you to contend earnestly for the faith which was once for all delivered to the saints. For certain men have crept in unnoticed, who long ago were marked out for this condemnation, ungodly men, who turn the grace of our God into lewdness and deny the only Lord God and our Lord Jesus Christ." (Jude 1: 3-4)

Mike Bickle said, *"The number one threat in the church is false teachers in the body of Christ."* (From the sermon series "Discerning Truth and Error about God's Grace")

True Discernment or Internet Goofiness

In our attempt to avoid false teachers and false teaching, I would encourage us all to try to avoid the internet as our source as much as possible. Those that feel they are called to expose the evils of heresy with their various websites are a dime a dozen on the internet. I believe it is unhealthy to spend time listening to the, often extreme, negativity of some. The problem is they often lump together the good solid teachers in the body of Christ and with those who are obviously false and dangerous. I actually saw someone the other day that mentioned Billy Graham was a false prophet.

I believe we should never speak against, publicly or privately, any church or ministry, no matter how "off" they seem to be. To do this, I believe, is to risk grieving the Holy Spirit. It is fine to point out a particular false teaching, but I believe we should not be naming names. There are those who would vehemently disagree with me on this. All I know is that scripture is clear about how we are to honor one another. I am also very aware of what the Lord himself has said to me about this. He told me not to go there. I know many on the internet feel they have a "call from God" to expose evil. With this kind of criticism, it is possible to release demonic curses upon the people that are spoken against, even if the person doing the criticizing is unaware of it.

It is much better to develop a positive spirit of discernment, rooted in the Holy Spirit, than to be overly judgmental of all kinds of ministries. We will always have false teachers and false teaching. Wisdom would suggest that it is much more beneficial to familiarize ourselves with the real than to focus on the false.

It's interesting how they train people in banks to recognize counterfeit money. They don't put them in a room with a bunch of counterfeit money and train them on how to be familiar with it. What they do is put people in a room with the real thing until they become so familiar with the genuine that they will recognize the false every time. Let's give ourselves to pursuing the true and the genuine in the kingdom of God and we will have proper discernment based on love, patience and humility. We need to learn to trust the Spirit of Truth.

*"However, when He, the **Spirit of truth**, has come, He will **guide you into all truth**; for He will not speak on His own authority, but*

whatever He hears He will speak; and He will tell you things to come."
(John 16:13)

The Power of Commitment

In developing a burning heart of passion for the Lord, we need to be a person of commitment. In this life there are any number of worthy causes, activities and purposes that we could commit to. In the western world we tend to compartmentalize our obligations. Along with family, job, school, recreation and a number of other things, we can easily make Jesus just another one of our compartments. In our commitment to God, He must be the umbrella over our entire life.

Committing to God is the understanding that our lives are not our own, but we are bought with a price. (1 Corinthians 6:19-20) It is the walking out of denying yourself and taking up your cross and following Him. (Matthew 16:24) It is the revelation of losing my life for Him and then, ultimately, finding it. (Matthew 10:39) Our commitment to Jesus, no matter what it costs us, will ultimately translate into eternal glory with Him. (Romans 8:18)

Ultimately, our reason for committing to God is that He is fully worthy of our complete devotion and commitment. He gave everything for me, why then in turn should I not give everything for Him? The dictionary definition of commit is to: *Pledge or dedicate to a course, policy, or use. Commit oneself to resolve to remain in a long-term emotional relationship with someone.* (Oxford)

Committing To the Lord

Psalms 37:5 says, *"Commit your way to the LORD, Trust also in Him, And He shall bring it to pass."* The Hebrew word in the Strong's concordance for **"commit"** is **"galal"** which is: *to roll, commit, remove, roll (away, down, together), run down, seek occasion, trust, wallow.* The idea is to be so totally wrapped up in God that you almost can't tell where one starts and the other leaves off. The word **"way"** is the Hebrew word "derek" which means; *a road (as trodden); figuratively a course of life or mode of action.* (Strong's) The thought here is that the commitment we made to follow Jesus is a life path chosen that we must never deviate from. Commitment to the Lord is crucial, especially when that straight and narrow path we walk becomes steep and rough. We must resolve to continue to walk with Jesus no matter what.

What Are the Benefits of a Committed Life?

The first benefit is the great honor and privilege of laying down your life for Jesus. Jesus said in Matthew 10:39, *"He who finds his life will lose it, and he who loses his life for My sake will find it."* Having a committed heart is one of the ways that we truly find our life in Him. Oftentimes commitment is not easy or fun, but it is always worth it.

The next benefit of commitment is that it paves the way for others to be touched and healed. I've seen those who were committed to staying after a meeting to pray for people when it would have been much easier to just leave and go have a meal. Their commitment to serving God created an opportunity for others to be touched by God. John spoke of this commitment in 1 John 3:16. He spoke of laying down of our lives as we follow

Jesus as our example. *"By this we know love, because He laid down His life for us. And we also ought to lay down our lives for the brethren."*

The next benefit of commitment is that it brings a deep inner joy in serving our great King. The joy comes in relationship, not religious duty. Choosing to live a life serving God produces the outcome of a heart relationship with Jesus. It is then that we find our commitment to Him is a result of an overwhelmingly obvious choice to follow Him because He is so worthy, not because we are trying to earn something. There is great joy in being free from religious positioning and striving for advancement. There is great contentment in just being wherever you are with Him.

The final benefit of our commitment to Jesus will come at the end of our earthly life. The thought that someday we get to stand before Him and hear the words, *"Well done good and faithful servant"* should be a great encouragement to us. (Matthew 25:23) As long as we all are here on this earth; we will have some enduring trials to walk through. The thought that no matter what we endure and suffer for Him in this life, it will be turned to pure joy and reward for eternity. There will be no regrets to those who live a committed life pleasing to God. You may say to yourself, "I have been living the Christian life but I haven't been that committed. What do I do?" You first must realize that it is not about determining to do better; it's about a heart choice to serve Him because you love Him. There is great reward ahead for those who choose this life. (Revelation 22:12) Choose in your heart to follow hard after him from this day forward.

Passion - Fuel for the Flame

At the heart of the burning flame that God has given us for Himself is passion. One of the Hebrew words for **"passion"** is *"patho."* It is the root of positive words like empathy and sympathy and negative words like apathy, pathetic and pathological. Patho means; *to experience a sensation or impression (usually painful): - feel, passion, suffer, vex.* (Strong's) Passion means that you love someone so much that you are instantly willing to suffer and possibly die for them. It is the love that a parent is to have for their child, a spouse is to have for their mate and human beings are to have for their God. It is also exactly what Jesus had for us in suffering on the cross. He was willing to sacrifice, for the first time, His relationship with the Father, by taking our sin upon Himself. It was passion for us that enabled Him to endure this, because we are the joy that was set before Him. (Hebrews12:2)

Much of the Psalms is an expression of heart passion for God. Like the longing in Psalms 63:1, *"O God, You are my God; Early will I seek You; My soul thirsts for You; My flesh longs for You In a dry and thirsty land Where there is no water."* Psalms 107:9, *"For He satisfies the longing soul, and fills the hungry soul with goodness.* The thirsting in Psalms 42:2 *My soul thirsts for God, for the living God. When shall I come and appear before God?"* and Psalms 63:8 *"My soul thirsts for God, for the living God. When shall I come and appear before God?"* And the desire of Psalms 73:25 *"Whom have I in heaven but You? And there is none upon earth that I desire besides You."*

The Burning Heart, Passion and Prayer

How can I pray passionately like the master? How can I be a person of prayer whom God can use in this day? Where do I even begin? First you must have the same sense of desperation that the disciples had when they asked, "Lord, teach us to pray." (Luke 11:1) This desperation is reflected in Jeremiah 29:13 *"And you will seek Me and find Me, when you search for Me with **all your heart**."*

It would seem that as the disciples compared their prayer life to that of Jesus, they came up glaringly short. The encouraging aspect of this is that it spurred them to ask. Many would have said, "OH I could never pray like that so I won't even try." No; they asked to be taught. They humbled themselves and admitted their weakness. Of course, He immediately responded and began to teach them.

Next, we must enter the heart of Jesus in order to pray with His passion. This means dying to our own ideas, our own opinions and what seems important to us at the time. It all must be surrendered to Him. We need to have His same mind. In Philippians 2:5-8 we read; *"Let this mind be in you which was also in Christ Jesus, who, being in the form of God, did not consider it robbery to be equal with God, but made Himself of no reputation, taking the form of a bondservant, and coming in the likeness of men. And being found in appearance as a man, He humbled Himself and became obedient to the point of death, even the death of the cross."*

When we talk about praying with passion, we are not just referring to volume or even someone with a loud, boisterous personality. It is possible to pray passionately and quietly at the same time. It is not volume but intensity that makes the difference. Do you know that you can pray passionately in your house early in the morning with other people sleeping? Even with whispered tones you can pray passionately. You can also cup your hands and clap to the Lord without making hardly a sound. The idea is passion, focus and fervency, not just volume. There are definitely times to be loud, but it doesn't have to be always.

We are talking about praying with the passion and compassion of Jesus. In James 5:16 we read that, **"the effectual fervent prayer of a righteous man avails much."** (KJV) The words "fervent prayer" in the Greek is the word "energeo" (obviously where we get the word energy from) which means *"to be mighty in."* The words "avails much" are the Greek words "Ischuo" and "Polos" which together mean *"to exercise force on a large scale."* (Strong's) The idea is that fervent prayer makes much power available. As we pray fervently, with passion, the power of the Holy Spirit is released. In other types of prayer, it is perfectly fine to pray in subdued tones. However, in intercession there must be passion.

Persevering Prayer

The whole point of intercession is to pray in a way that will move the heart of God. I love the old acronym P.U.S.H. Pray Until Something Happens. Back in my early days as a believer in the 1970s, we referred to this as "praying through." Unfortunately, I think today this concept may be falling through the cracks of our busy, high paced lives. Persevering prayer is the whole point of the parable Jesus told in Luke 18:1-8. *"Then He spoke a parable to them, that men always ought to pray and not lose heart, saying: 'There was in a certain city a judge who did not fear God nor regard man. Now there was a widow in that city; and she came to him, saying, 'Get justice for me from my adversary.' And he would not for a while; but afterward he said within himself, 'Though I do not fear God nor regard man, yet because this widow troubles me I will avenge her, lest by her continual coming she weary me.' Then the Lord said, 'Hear what the unjust judge said. And shall God not avenge His own elect who cry out day and night to Him, though He bears long with them? I tell you that He will avenge them speedily. Nevertheless, when the Son of Man comes, will He really find faith on the earth?'"*

The whole impetus of these verses is captured in the first verse as Jesus is introducing the parable; ***"men always ought to pray and not lose heart."*** Perseverance is also spoken of in Ephesians 6:18, *"praying always with all prayer and supplication in the Spirit, being watchful to this end with all perseverance and supplication for all the saints."* and Luke 11:9 *"So I say to you, ask, and it will be given to you; seek, and you will find knock, and it will be opened to you."*

God's heart is moved by desperate, passionate, persevering prayer. It is prayer that will give us an audience with the King and access to his Heart.

Entering the Heart of Jesus

The key to hearing God's heart is getting in touch with His voice. It is the privilege of every believer to hear the voice of God resounding deep in their heart. Jesus said in John 10:4, *"…when he puts forth his own sheep, he goes before them, and the sheep follow him: **for they know his voice.**"* This also means tapping into the endless stream of thoughts that God has for us. This thought stream is described in Psalm 40:5, *"Many, O LORD my God, are Your wonderful works Which You have done; And Your thoughts toward us cannot be recounted to You in order; If I would declare and speak of them, they are more than can be numbered."*

I believe this story about John G. Lake says it all:

*"During the later years of his life, John G. Lake received a powerful angelic visitation. In this encounter, the angel opened the scriptures to the Book of Acts saying, "This is Pentecost as God gave it through the **heart of Jesus**. Strive for this...contend for this...teach the people to pray for this. For this, and this alone will meet the necessity of the human heart and this alone will have power to overcome the forces of darkness." As the angel departed he admonished Brother Lake insisting, **"Pray, pray, pray**...Teach the people to pray. **Prayer and prayer alone, much prayer, persistent prayer is the door of entrance to the heart of God."*** (From article "Anointed for Revival", 1995, Brisbane, Australia by Liz Godschalk)

As we enter through this door, we will find His immense heart that beats passionately for every last human on earth. We will find ourselves lost in the ocean of His great care and compassion. In that place, we come to the conclusion that all that matters is Jesus. All the stuff of our lives begins to lose its demanding priority, and we realize that God receiving what is His heart's desire is what really counts. In this, prayer moves from being an option to an absolute must. We must "pray, pray, pray."

You Are the Result of Passionate Prayer

You are saved today because someone prayed for you. God loved you so much that He gave someone the piece of His heart that was extended in love for you. Then they prayed that back to Him and the Holy Spirit was released to draw you to Jesus. The Lord has a desperate love for the unsaved. One day He illustrated it to me like this; in the mist of praying for the lost He asked me this question. "How would you feel if one of your kids had been kidnapped and you could find no one to help you get them back? Would you be desperate?" I thought of my 5 kids, two of whom almost died at birth, and I said to Him, "Lord I can't even begin to imagine."

I know this would relate to sharing Jesus with people, but it also has to do with that which precedes evangelism; and that is intercession. I received my first lesson in the power of prayer relating to evangelism in college. I began at a secular college with a desire to see people come to Jesus, so I asked God what He wanted me to do. He told me to begin to pray for this girl that I had in a writing class I was taking. He said I was not to share with her but I was only to pray. So I put her on the top of my prayer list.

Soon after, a friend of mine told me that he had begun to share Jesus with a girl on campus. He said he had invited her to church but she didn't want to go. Then about a week later she said she would go to church, but when the altar call was given she didn't respond. My friend was very discouraged. Then one day he grabbed me on campus and said that he had taken her to church again and she was gloriously saved. I said, "Wow that's great news! Oh, by the way what is this girl's name?" When he told me her name I couldn't believe what I was hearing. It was the same girl I had been praying for every day for over a month! Rather incredible considering the enrollment of that college was over 10,000 students. God had used my friend to witness, and me to pray. The end result was a new believer in the kingdom. Jesus has great passion for every person on earth. He wants to give us His passion in prayer.

Our Ultimate Example – Jesus

Finally, in praying with passion we must follow the example of Jesus and die to self. These verses demonstrate this fact.

"Let this mind be in you which was also in Christ Jesus, who, being in the form of God, did not consider it robbery to be equal with God, but made Himself of no reputation, taking the form of a bondservant, and coming in the likeness of men. And being found in appearance as a man, He humbled Himself and became obedient to the point of death, even the death of the cross." (Philippians 2:5-8)

"Then Jesus said to His disciples, 'If anyone desires to come after Me, let him deny himself, and take up his cross, and follow Me. For whoever desires to save his life will lose it, but whoever loses his life for My sake will find it.'" (Matthew 16:24-25)

"Most assuredly, I say to you, unless a grain of wheat falls into the ground and dies, it remains alone; but if it dies, it produces much grain. He who loves his life will lose it, and he who hates his life in this world will keep it for eternal life. If anyone serves Me, let him

follow Me; and where I am, there My servant will be also. If anyone serves Me, him My Father will honor." (John 12:24-26)

If you haven't already discovered it, your flesh doesn't want to pray. Our carnal nature (self) wants nothing to do with sacrificial intercession. For one thing, there is no recognition in it. (Matthew 6:5, 6) The flesh loves the spotlight and hates the closet. Then there is the whole area of discipline. Our selfish nature loves comfort at all cost. The story of Jesus and the disciples praying in the garden is our prime example of this point. *"Then He came to the disciples and found them sleeping, and said to Peter, "What! Could you not watch with Me one hour? Watch and pray, lest you enter into temptation. The spirit indeed is willing, but the flesh is weak."* (Matthew 26:40-41)

God is extremely passionate about his creation, especially about human beings whom the life of Jesus was given for. It is interesting that the times Jesus shows the most passion is always connected to prayer.

First in the temple; Matthew 21:12-13 *"Then Jesus went into the temple of God and drove out all those who bought and sold in the temple, and overturned the tables of the money changers and the seats of those who sold doves. And He said to them, 'It is written, My house shall be called a house of prayer, but you have made it a den of thieves.'"* Then in John 2:17 *"Then His disciples remembered that it was written, 'Zeal for Your house has eaten Me up.'"*

The next instance is at the tomb of Lazarus; John 11:41-43 *"Then they took away the stone from the place where the dead man was lying.*

And Jesus lifted up His eyes and said, 'Father, I thank You that You have heard Me. And I know that You always hear Me, but because of the people who are standing by I said this, that they may believe that You sent Me.' Now when He had said these things, He cried with a loud voice, 'Lazarus, come forth!'"

Then in the Garden of Gethsemane; Matthew 26:39-41 "He went a little farther and fell on His face, and prayed, saying, 'O My Father, if it is possible, let this cup pass from Me; nevertheless, not as I will, but as You will.' Then He came to the disciples and found them sleeping, and said to Peter, 'What! Could you not watch with Me one hour? Watch and pray, lest you enter into temptation. The spirit indeed is willing, but the flesh is weak.'"

Then ultimately on the cross; Mark 15:34 "And at the ninth hour Jesus cried out with a loud voice, saying, 'Eloi, Eloi, lama sabachthani?' which is translated, 'My God, My God, why have You forsaken Me?'"

It was His passion for us that gave Jesus the resolve to endure the cross. Thus the declaration in Hebrews 12:2 "looking unto Jesus, the author and finisher of our faith, who for the joy that was set before Him endured the cross, despising the shame, and has sat down at the right hand of the throne of God."

Final Thought - The process of allowing God to give us a burning heart that is like His heart is crucial for us to be effective in intercession. This song, "Children of the Burning Heart" from Steven Curtis Chapman says it best:

We were the dreamers, the boys on the wild frontier
The new believers with nothing in the world to fear
We had discovered the treasure of the
love and the grace of God
And it burned like a fire in our hearts, and we would...
Throw back our heads and run with the passion
Through the fields of forgiveness and grace
We carried the eternal flame
With an undying hope and a blazing conviction
Of a truth that would never fade
We were glowing in the dark
Children of the burning heart
And now for the dreamers, and those
who have dared to believe
The flames call us deeper into the great mystery
For as we draw near to the Father we
are lost in this one desire
To be wholly consumed by His fire, so let us...
Throw back our heads and run with the passion
Through the fields of forgiveness and grace
We carry the eternal flame
With an undying hope and a blazing conviction
Of a truth that will never die
We are glowing in the dark.

Chapter 6

PRAYING FOR JUSTICE, RESTORATION AND RESTITUTION

I am about to share with you what I believe to be one of the most vital and important revelations I have received from the Lord about prayer. The reason I say that it is about prayer, and not just about intercession, is that it includes not just praying for others, but praying for ourselves as well. Nonetheless, it is an awesome and powerful tool in intercession.

This revelation has become a life message for me. If you were to ask me what one revelation, I would like to share with a group of people, this would be it. I have shared this message publicly numerous times. God has been using this revelation to touch many lives. I believe when the Holy Spirit teaches us and gives us revelation, it is not just so we can have the knowledge of something, it is so we can live in the life of it. This is how the Word of Christ dwells in us richly. This revelation didn't come as I sat quietly in my study. I lived it out as He showed it to me. Let me tell you the story…

The Prophetic "Oregon Trail"

In the year 2000, Darla and I did a "one-way vacation" across country with five children. We moved 3,000 miles from Springfield, Oregon to Asheville, North Carolina at the word of the Lord. Along with that word came numerous confirmations that this was God's path for us. I remember Pastor Frank Damazio talking to me when he heard that I was thinking about going. He said, "You know, you have to have at least three major confirmations to make a move like this." I said, "I have that." Then he said, "Okay, seven." We both laughed. We lived in Asheville for many years and it was an amazing adventure. In August of 2006, Darla and I, along with our youngest daughter, Jessica made plans to go back to Oregon for a visit and for Darla and I to attend our 30th high school class reunion in our home town of Cottage Grove. We had planned to stay there about two weeks with my folks.

About three days before we left for Oregon, I was meeting with a group of intercessors in our church. They told me that they believed the Lord had shown them that I was going to receive some of my inheritance on this trip. I told them that I wasn't aware of any, but I would be open. The morning we were to leave for the airport, I was at the church praying. I was about to leave when the Lord impressed me to go into the church bookstore. When I went into the bookstore, He showed me a book that I was to take for the trip. The book was called, *"The Books of Destiny"* by Paul Keith Davis. Once on the plane, I began to read. Although the revelation of **Justice, Restoration and Restitution** (JRR for short) isn't directly given in this book, God did use it powerfully to get me on track for what was to come.

As I read the book, the Lord told me that He was going to highlight certain words and when He did, I was to write that word in my journal. The first word was **justice**. The Lord told me to remember that word, so I wrote it down. It was the same with the words **restoration** and **restitution**. I can show you in my journal where I first wrote those three words together. It was a "kairos" moment for me. As we began our final approach to the Portland airport, the Lord began to speak to my heart. He said, **"I have an assignment for you while you are in Oregon. I want you to get up early each morning and go to the places I show you. When you get there, I want you to ask Me for Justice, Restoration and Restitution for all that the enemy has stolen from you in that place."** The first morning there I was wide awake at 5:30am. West coast time is three hours earlier than east coast, so it was easy to get up. I asked the Lord where He wanted me to go and He directed me to go to the place where my High School used to be. The building had been torn down and there was nothing but a soccer field now. It didn't matter. I prayed anyway. I said, "Lord please, You are going to have to help me. I don't exactly know what to do." He said with a determined voice, **"Just ask Me."** I asked, "Is it that simple?" He said, "It's that simple!"

I could remember many hard times in high school when the enemy tormented me with fear, inferiority and temptation. But on the other hand, it was during that time that I came to know Jesus. So I stood on that ground, early in the morning, and said for the first time, "Lord I ask for **Justice, Restoration and Restitution** for all that the enemy took from me in this place." As I prayed I could feel God's power being released against the enemy. I could sense things breaking loose in the spiritual realm. It was awesome. Thus began the early morning adventures of going from place to place in the land of my youth. I went to my grade school, my junior high, places that I had lived, wherever God would direct me to go.

The next part of the story involves, what is called, "Seeing in the Spirit." I know it sounds a bit "New Age," but I believe they took the idea of seeing spiritual things from us. Bill Johnson said, *"Many of us have thought that the ability to see into the spiritual realm is more the result of a special gift than an unused potential of everyone."*

One morning I went to a place where I spent a lot of time in my twenties and early thirties. It was six o'clock in the morning and I asked the Lord what He wanted me to do. He told me to walk up to the front door. Being early in the morning, I thought it unlikely that anyone would be around. I stood before the closed door and asked for **Justice, Restoration and Restitution** for all the enemy had stolen from me in that place. He told me to look into the spiritual realm and see what was in the building. As I closed my eyes and looked into the spiritual realm, I was aware of two angels standing with me.

Then I looked through the doors into the center of a large room. I saw there what appeared to be a glass museum display case. Inside the case was a sword, a mantle and a pair of binoculars. I asked the Lord about what I was seeing and He said, "Those are yours. The enemy took them from you almost twenty years ago." I said, "What do You want me to do." He said, "Go get them." So in my spiritual imagination, the two angels and I went through the front door into the center of the room. Then one of the angels went over to the case and ripped the glass cover off. I reached down and took the sword, the mantle and the binoculars. As I did, I became aware of angry demonic forces around us and the Lord said. "You need to leave this building now." Once back outside the door, the Lord said, "Get off the property now." So within seconds I was back on the city street in front of the building. The difference was that now I had the spiritual gifts of a sword, a mantle and binoculars that had been returned to me. The scope, magnitude and thrill of the adventure were increasing.

I know this may sound a bit strange, but I am telling you the story just as it happened. I understand in telling stories, there is a tendency to embellish facts. In this telling I have endeavored not to do so. In this journey, my heart's cry was just to be led by the Holy Spirit.

I would like to tell you one more story. I took a drive out of town to a little community called London Springs, where I lived until I was thirteen. I stopped at a few places and prayed the prayer. It was a great place to grow up, but there was some harsh times of fear and rejection the Lord wanted to deal with.

One of the places I stopped was my old elementary school. As I walked to the playground I instantly remembered difficult times of having to deal with a couple of bullies in my school. These guys were very useful to the enemy in allowing me to become fearful and self-doubting. They definitely played a part in me developing an orphan mindset. Our enemy has all the negative qualities of a bully. He tries to intimidate us, instill fear in us and lie to us to get us to think that we are something less. In dealing with a bully there are several possible courses of action. One is to stand up to him and let him know that you will no longer submit to his abuse. However, the most likely solution is to go to a higher authority that can deal with and stop the bullying. In JRR we are confronting the enemy and, at the same time, calling upon the ultimate authority to deal with the fear, the intimidation and the lies.

About the time I thought I was through, I heard the Lord encourage me to keep driving. I was about 17 miles out of town, driving along what is called "Big River" when I heard the Holy Spirit say, "Stop." I got out at a place along the river where we used to go swimming when I was a young child. As I stood on the rocks next to the rapids I remembered the story that I was told about something that happened to me in that place. At that very spot, when I was about two years old, I somehow fell into the water. I began to float downstream, facedown like a piece of wood, when my Dad looked over and saw me. He jumped in and pulled me out of the water and I took a deep breath and began to wail. For many years after, I was very afraid of water. I asked the Holy Spirit why He was reminding me of this and He said, **"The enemy tried to kill you at this place when you were two years old and there has been a spirit of death attached to your life ever since."**

All of a sudden it was like all the lights came on. I thought of all the death I had experienced. My fourteen-year-old brother, David, was killed on his motorcycle when I was sixteen. I didn't think about it until later, that I was supposed to be on the back of that motorcycle, but I changed my mind about going with him at the last second for no apparent reason.

Darla, and I went through having a stillbirth, four miscarriages and almost lost the two daughters we did have naturally during and immediately following their births. I saw it clearly; the spirit of death had been ripping me off all my life. So I asked the Holy Spirit, "What should I do?" And He said with an impassioned, determined voice, **"Just ask Me!"** So through hot tears I asked for **Justice, Restoration and Restitution** for all that the enemy had stolen from me in that place. I could feel shock waves in the spirit. **The spirit of death was totally defeated.** To this day I cannot share this story without being moved to tears. Oh and by the way, the name of the swimming hole was called, **"Dead Man's Hole."**

Kristi's Story

Somehow, in that encounter by the river, I knew that if this spirit of death had not been dealt with, it would have been passed on in my family line. It is most likely that our kids would've had trouble having children as well. But something marvelous happened relating to our daughter Kristi, whom we adopted when she was 11 years old. All of her childhood she wanted nothing more than to grow up someday and be a mother. When she was a teenager, three doctors told her that she could never have children because of the abuse she suffered at the hands of her natural father. This news ultimately caused her to rebel against God and eventually leave our home at the age of 17. For several years she lived a very worldly lifestyle. She ended up in a relationship with a young man who also was a backslidden Christian. During the relationship she became pregnant. She knew that she was not supposed to be able to carry the child and was fearful of a miscarriage. But the miscarriage never came. She told us weeping on the phone that she was going to have a baby. God restored her to Himself and to us. Now, she is not only the mother of one child, but of three wonderful sons. Three sons for the three doctors that told her she would never have children. Of course, Dr. Jesus had yet to weigh in on that prognosis. God is all about working in impossible situations to bring **Justice, Restoration and Restitution.**

An Unexpected Inheritance

Remember the prophetic word from the intercessors that I had received before my Oregon trip? Well the last day of the trip, my mother came out with a box of old items that have been in the family for years. My parents gave me a bag of old coins and some cut glass jewels that came from Europe with my ancestors. The jewels are around 130 years old, and the oldest coin is from 1737. I believe these are a tangible sign from God to confirm the word of **Justice, Restoration and Restitution**.

Pre-emptive Wisdom

Before we look into how to pray for Justice, Restoration and Restitution, I think we need to say something about stopping the enemy before he gets started. One of the mindsets we need to renounce is that which says "whatever the enemy dishes out we just have to accept it." We don't have to keep putting up with whatever he does in our lives. God wants us to understand that when the enemy comes to steal, we can rise up and say no. In our everyday life we don't just lie down and let someone take from us and offer no resistance, do we? James said, *"Therefore submit to God. **Resist** the devil and he will flee from you."* (James 4:7) Peter said, *"Be sober, be vigilant; because your adversary the devil walks about like a roaring lion, seeking whom he may devour. **Resist*** *him...*" (1Peter 5:8, 9) I believe if we have an opportunity to resist the enemy, we should. But often times he has stolen from us almost before we are aware of it. If we find ourselves having been stolen from, the good news is that we can do something about it. We can ask the Lord for justice.

> *"The thief does not come except to steal, and to kill, and to destroy. I have come that they may have life, and that they may have it more abundantly."* (John 10:10)

The Lords Justice

To fully grasp this revelation, we must have an understanding of the Lord's justice. When we talk about the justice of God, we need to picture in our mind two settings in heaven. The first is a courtroom setting and the second is the throne room of God. In the natural world there are many who have injustice forced upon them and they have no recourse. In the kingdom of God, one of the benefits we have is that we can bring our case before the courtroom of heaven. We have an invitation to come boldly and cast our cares before the heavenly judge who is also the king of the universe. God loves you so much that, not only does He know about the enemy stealing from you, He is very passionate about doing something about it.

Hebrews 4:16 invites us to; *"come **boldly** to the **throne of grace**, that we may obtain mercy and find grace to help in time of need."* We have an invitation to have an audience with, not only our just judge, but our great king. He has all authority to do something about the injustice that the enemy has wrought in our lives and the lives of others. The throne we are invited to is the throne of grace. The word "grace" in the Greek here is "charis." By definition we are called to the throne of His gratifying graciousness manifested through the divine influence upon the heart. It is the throne of His acceptance, benefit, favor, gift, joy, liberality, pleasure, thanksgiving and worthiness.

Justice begins with a Ruling from the Bench

*"I was watching; and the same horn was making war against the saints, **and prevailing against them**, until the Ancient of Days came, and **a judgment was made in favor of the saints of the Most High**, and the time came for the saints to possess the kingdom."* (Daniel 7:21-22)

*"Then the one who had been living forever came and **pronounced judgment in favor** of the people of the Supreme God. The time had arrived for God's people to receive royal power."* (Daniel 7:22 GNB)

The word *judgment* is from the Hebrew words *diŷndûn*, which means to rule, by implication, to judge (as umpire); and *mishpaṭ* which means properly a verdict (favorable or unfavorable) pronounced judicially. (Strong's) One scene is a judge, after hearing all the evidence, making a ruling from the bench and handing down a verdict. Another scene is a king who makes a decree and, when He speaks, it is law and must be carried out.

In JRR we go before the judge of heaven and bring our case. He then rules in our favor as the gavel comes down and justice is rendered.

"And he shall judge the world in righteousness; he shall minister judgment to the people in uprightness." (Psalms 9:8)

Judgment and Justice

The words **judgment** and **justice** appear side by side in scripture **twenty times.** Judgment is that which ushers in justice. There cannot be one without the other. In scripture justice means being brought into rightness. In Webster's Dictionary it means "The virtue which consists in giving to everyone what is his due." This is demonstrated in these verses:

*"Behold, the days come, saith the LORD, that I will raise unto David a righteous Branch, and a King shall reign and prosper, and shall **execute judgment and justice** in the earth."*
(Jeremiah 23:5 KJV)

*"I, the LORD, **love justice**! But I hate robbery and injustice. My people, I solemnly promise to reward you with an eternal agreement."* (Isaiah 61:8)

Established in God's Throne

The justice of God is so much a part of His nature that it constitutes the substance of the throne. God rules from His throne in justice. That is the reason no human being can shake their fists at God and accuse Him of being unjust. If we ever think God is unjust, it is only because we can't see the whole picture. It is guaranteed that there will be absolute justice on every spirit of darkness for their thievery and destruction on mankind.

"Righteousness and justice are the foundation of Your throne; Mercy and truth go before Your face." (Psalms 89:14)

"Clouds and darkness are round about him: Righteousness and justice are the foundation of his throne." (Psalms 97:2 ASV)

Here is a quote from *"Books of Destiny"* by Paul Keith Davis:

"We have not fully embraced the justice of heaven because we do not understand its absolute application. However, the Lord's justice will unleash an end-time army of believers equipped with the resources of heaven. When He reveals Himself as the Just Judge, a verdict will be rendered in favor of the saints. All valuable callings, anointing's, commissions and gifts entrusted to God's people throughout the ages will be restored and redeemed. Divine justice renders blessings on behalf of the righteous and judgment upon unrighteousness. Justice restores what has been stolen and compensates the victim when the thief has been captured. Almost every believer can testify that he or she has been stolen from. For many, their children and family members have been inflicted with illnesses and hardships. Others have had finances devoured. Much of the spiritual inheritance entrusted to God's people has been unlawfully taken. Precious ministry gifts and spiritual anointing's have been lost through incursions of demonic 'bandits'. He will recover and amplify everything the enemy has attempted to devour and destroy."

In the natural, all of us probably remember a time when someone stole from us or destroyed something that was ours. Remember how it made you feel when you realized you had been stolen from. Of all the emotions, such as anger or sadness, the feeling that we probably remember the most is a strong sense of injustice. Let's take it to another level. It is one thing if you steal from me but another thing altogether if you steal from one of my kids. This is what God's heart is like in your situation. He strongly desires to bring justice, restoration and restitution into the areas of life where the enemy has stolen from you. God's heart is stirred about the stealing and killing and destroying that the enemy has been up to in your life. He is not only willing, but is extremely able to do something about it.

The End Result of Justice - a Process in Order

Ultimately, when justice is accomplished it brings two primary outcomes. When the ruling is given, it opens the way for restoration and restitution. Once, when I was praying this prayer out, I got the order wrong, I said, "Lord I ask for justice, restitution and restoration. **The Holy Spirit said "Stop, you have to get the order right. It is Justice, Restoration and Restitution."**

For a while I didn't understand why. But now I know it is because those three words describe a whole, completed process. It is not enough just to ask for justice. I have heard a lot of people pray for the justice of God, but it is just the first step. We must see it through to the end, which is restitution. Have you ever heard of a court situation where someone receives a judgment that they will have "x" amount of dollars paid to them, and for some reason they never seem to get paid? Whether it is because of endless appeals, or the other party files for bankruptcy, something happens. In our earthly courts, the judge leaves it up to someone else to make sure the money is paid.

In the heavenly court, the judge Himself directly oversees the reacquisition of what was stolen. This judge, our Father God, also personally demands that the caught thief repay us seven times the value. He takes back that which was originally stolen (Restoration) and demands repayment of seven times the value of that which was original stolen. (Restitution) This is the equation:

Justice + Restoration + Restitution =
Reacquisition of the Original x 7

*"Men do not despise a thief, if he steals to satisfy his soul when he is hungry; But if he be found, he shall **restore sevenfold**; he shall give all the substance of his house."* (Proverbs 6:30-31)

*"And **I will restore** to you the years that the locust hath eaten."* (Joel 2:25)

*"Dearly beloved, avenge not yourselves, but rather give place unto wrath: for it is written, Vengeance is mine; **I will repay**, says the Lord."* (Romans 12:19)

*"Strengthen the weak hands, and make firm the feeble knees. Say to those who are fearful-hearted, be strong, do not fear! Behold, **your God will come with vengeance, with the recompense of God**; He will come and save you."* (Isaiah 35:3-4)

*"Energize the limp hands, strengthen the rubbery knees. Tell fearful souls, 'Courage! Take heart! **God is here, right here, on his way to put things right** and redress all wrongs. He's on his way! He'll save you!'"* (Isaiah 35:3-4 Message)

This revelation of **Justice, Restoration and Restitution** deals directly with demonic larceny against human kind. As we pray, the "thief is caught" and God reacquires and releases the seven-fold blessing of that which was taken. There has been so much the enemy has stolen, and I believe God, in His justice and His love for His children, wants it returned. God wants us to ask Him to restore and bring restitution. One of our big problems is that, typically, we just don't ask God for much. We might have shame, inferiority or an orphan mindset. But often we just don't ask. Actually, many of us have been trained not to ask. How many of you, as you were growing up, were told, "Now when you go over to the neighbor's house, don't be asking for things." We are trained not to go and look in their refrigerator or rifle through their cupboards. And rightly so; nothing is more bothersome than a neighbor kid who is always asking for something. The problem arises, though, when we see ourselves as a visitor in God's house instead of one of His kids. I don't know about you, but my kids don't hesitate to ask me for something they want. **God wants, wants, wants, and wants** us to ask him for Justice, Restoration and Restitution.

Restoration is defined in scripture as: *to turn back, return to the starting point, to be safe, completed, make amends, to ascend, to reconstitute, to give up, give over, give back, complete thoroughly and repair.* In Webster's it is defined: *to return to a person, as a specific thing which he has lost, or which has been taken from him and unjustly detained. We restore lost or stolen goods to the owner.*

Restitution is defined in scripture as: *compensation, reconstitution (in health, home or organization)* In Webster's it is defined: *The act of making good, or of giving an equivalent for any loss, damage or injury.* Then as we pray, if it comes out of our heart of total surrender to His will, it will also release an upwards of a 100-fold blessing.

"And Jesus answered and said, Verily I say unto you, there is no man that hath left house, or brethren, or sisters, or father, or mother, or wife, or children, or lands, for my sake, and the gospel's, but he shall receive a **hundredfold** *now in this time, houses, and brethren, and sisters, and mothers, and children, and lands, with persecutions; and in the world to come eternal life."* (Mark 10:29-30)

Going Into the Enemy's Camp

Back in the 90s, we used to sing a worship chorus called, "Enemy's Camp." The lyrics go like this:

Well, I went to the enemy's camp and
I took back what he stole from me.

This is a great song and I have nothing to say against it. I would like to suggest, however, that instead of me going into the enemy's camp to get my stuff back, how about God Himself going in to retrieve it for me. If the enemy stole an apple from me, so to speak, and I went and took it back, the apple will probably have a worm in it, if you know what I mean. I would much rather have God, with all the legal backing of heaven, go and reacquire that which was stolen, check it all out and then come and give it to me, increased by seven times.

Is there a Limit?

You can apply this prayer to any area of life. The possibilities are endless. I heard someone once say, "The enemy hates you and has a terrible plan for your life." Anything the enemy has stolen, we can pray and ask God to have it returned. These are some of the areas you can pray for:

- Relationships
- Family members – family lines, back-slidden family members
- Healing – physical, emotional, mental
- Finances
- Callings, Ministries, Mantles
- Dreams about your Destiny
- Churches, Cities, Nations
- Salvation for the lost

Releasing Amazing Benefits

One of the first fruits of this prayer is the manifestation of actual blessings in the physical realm. It's not about wishful praying with little expectation of anything changing. It's about praying in faith and standing there until the answer is fully manifested.

When I prayed this prayer in Oregon, I received physical confirmation of the spiritual truth. Jesus said, *"When you pray and ask for something, believe that you have received it, and you will be given whatever you ask for."* (Mark 11:24 GNB)

The next benefit of this prayer is healed memories and emotions related to the incident. After about a week of praying this prayer in Cottage Grove, Oregon, I asked Darla one day, "Does it feel different to you being here this time?" She said, "Yes, it feels really good. It's amazing." I told her that after I would pray at a place, I was having a difficult time remembering the bad things related to that place in my past. It even felt as though the entire atmosphere of the town had changed.

The reigning demonic force over my home town has been the spirit of division. There have been loads of churches that were splits off of splits off of splits. Back in the 1800s the townspeople would feud and shoot at each other across the river. There is actually a river there named "The Row River." It was named after a "row" between two brothers-in-law which ended in murder. By this prayer, not only can God heal our memories, but He can change the very atmosphere of a place.

Then one day the Lord asked me this question, "What do you get when you shorten each of those words, **Just**ice **Rest**oration **Rest**itution? What you get is **Just Rest Rest.** The stress, turmoil, worry, anxiety, anger and resentment that many of these issues have caused has been almost overwhelming at times. God wants to release great rest into our lives and bring to an end us living under the heavy load of the enemy's emotional baggage. As this prayer is activated in your life, God brings with it great rest and peace. Many of God's people are laboring under a heavy weight placed there by an evil task master.

Much of my early days as a believer, I walked around with a knot of religious expectation in my gut. Today if I get a knot in my stomach, I stop and ask the Holy Spirit what is going on so we can deal with it. Our portion on earth should be love, joy, peace and rest.

"There remains therefore a rest to the people of God. For he that is entered into his rest, he also hath ceased from his own works, as God

did from his. Let us labor therefore to enter into that rest, lest any man fall after the same example of unbelief." (Hebrews 4:9-11)

How Is It Released?

In **Justice,** there is a release of **faith** required on our part, and a manifestation of the Father in declaring justice in the matter. In **Restoration,** there is a requirement of **trust** on our part, and a manifestation of Jesus in His restoring work of the Cross. Then in **Restitution, obedience** is required of us with a manifestation of the Holy Spirit working in our lives to bring restitution. This prayer is not a formula, but is released out of our relationship with the Father, the Son and the Holy Spirit.

Justice - Faith - Father
Restoration – Trust – Son
Restitution – Obedience – Holy Spirit

One day as I was praying this prayer, this phrase kept coming up as an "Amen" to the prayer... I said, "Lord let it be wholly, completely brought forth and released."

An Essential Component: Forgiveness

As I said before, for this process to work effectively we must be led by the Holy Spirit. To run out on our own can be fruitless and possibly dangerous. The first thing to be aware of is this; **this process will not work if you do not forgive every person involved.** I remember going to one of the places to pray JRR and I began to feel some of the past resentment coming back. The Holy Spirit spoke to me, **"For this prayer to work you must forgive everyone involved. You are never to pray Justice,**

Restoration and Restitution against any human being." To do so would be leveling a word curse against the person and would be equal with performing witchcraft. The next thing is that there is no room for fear, doubt or unbelief in this process. We must believe that God loves us and wants to answer our prayers.

Being Led by the Spirit

The key to effectively releasing this prayer is to be led by the Spirit. He will reveal the specific areas of our lives where the enemy has robbed from us. It is very important we understand that not everything bad that happens is from the enemy. There are often hard things the Lord allows in our lives to test us and purify us. But when the Lord reveals that it is definitely a work of the enemy, it is then we can ask Him for JRR with confidence.

Ask the Lord, where the places are He wants you to go and pray this prayer. If you can't actually travel to those places, just pray it out where you are. You do not have to strive in hearing the Lord about where to go and what to pray. It usually comes easy as we just submit to the Holy Spirit. If you have any questions about the Spirit's leading, wait for clarity and ask for confirmation. Here is a sample of how this prayer could be prayed. I have given this out as a card that many people keep in their Bible. Also, it is great to have on hand for praying in the Healing Rooms or in other ministry settings.

Praying Justice, Restoration And Restitution
- Lord, in this situation, I ask for your JUSTICE (Daniel 7:22)
- Lord, I ask you to bring RESTORATION (Joel 2:25)
- Lord, I ask you to release RESTITUTION (Acts 3:21)

- Lord, I forgive any people involved (Matthew 6:14)
- Lord, I ask back 7 times what was stolen (Proverbs 6:31)
- Lord, I ask to only remember the good (Philippians 4:8)
- Lord, I ask you to release JUST, REST, REST (Hebrews 4:9)

An Ongoing Blessing - JRR Testimonies

Since that trip to Oregon, I have prayed this prayer many times and shared the revelation with anyone who would listen. I have also received great reports of people who heard this message and, following the Spirit, went to places and prayed this prayer, and God moved powerfully. I heard one brother say that he prayed this prayer over a broken relationship and the relationship was restored to a place that, in his opinion, is seven times greater. It is powerful in intercession and hardly a day goes by that I don't pray it.

I was preparing to preach a word about Israel at a festival in Moravian Falls, North Carolina, when the Lord asked me how this word would apply to Israel and I was taken back. He showed me that Israel is barraged with possibly millions of word curses every day from the Muslim world. As I brought the word, I had everyone join me in praying **Justice, Restoration and Restitution** for Israel.

One of the things about this process is that God wants to unravel and undo the plans and plots of the enemy in our lives. This is demonstrated in the story of my good friend, Randall Martin, who upon hearing this revelation, asked the Lord where he was to go to pray it out. The Lord spoke to his heart and told him that he was to go to his high school and stand on the grounds and pray. Then the Lord told him something a bit unusual. He said that He was going to unravel all the work that the enemy had done in his life in that place, and as a prophetic demonstration of that, He wanted him to march around his high school backwards. This process is not a formula, but is birthed out of a relationship with the Holy Spirit. So Randall began to walk backwards, but felt foolish and stopped. Then the Lord said to him, "This is something that I want to do in your life, but it's up to you." So he responded to the Lord in faith and walked the entire circumference of his high school backwards. This may appear foolish in the natural realm, but in the spirit realm the Lord was unraveling and undoing the work of the enemy in his life.

Several years ago, another couple heard me preach this message and heard the Lord say that they were to pray about the fact that a spirit of poverty had somehow gotten into the family line. They went to the cemetery where their wealthy ancestors were buried and prayed out the prayer. A short time later they were going through some papers in the basement and a $10,000 bond fell out. This was something that they didn't even know they had.

One story that shows how the Spirit is using this message came just a few days after I had shared the JRR message at a recovery home group. I received the following e-mail:

Hello Mike,
I wanted to tell you what happened last Mon. I was asked to share my testimony at a drug awareness class. I had no idea where it was. I got

directions and proceeded to go. As I drove I asked God to give me peace because I was so nervous. As I turned on the road where the church is that they hold the meeting, I was shocked to see it was the very church parking lot where 7 years ago I parked my car to buy drugs from a trailer behind the church!

My heart began pounding. My thoughts began to race. I cried out to God. I can't believe I'm here again. I don't want to be here. A still small voice inside me said "justice, restoration and restitution". I began to pray the prayer you came to the house and shared. I mustered up the courage to walk into that church and gave my testimony. It's really all a blur.

After the meeting, the man who had asked me to come share came up to me. I had talked about being right there using drugs some 7 years ago. He thanked me for coming. Then said, " That man sitting in the third row at the meeting was the same man who lived in the trailer and sold you dope! He may still be dealing but not in our community. Your story had to affect him!" I immediately thanked God for this divine appointment. Whether it was for that dealer, I cannot say. But I can say that what Satan robbed me of that day 7 years ago, God fully restored to me the instant I prayed the prayer. Thank YOU for hearing the voice inside you that said to come to our house and share that message. God was and is using it to HIS Glory!

Beth

One of the great privileges of our time living in Scotland was to go and do on-site prayer and preach on the Isle of Lewis. We went to various places on the island and prayed during the day and were teaching, for the first time, what eventually became the Burning Heart's School of Intercession, in the evenings. We were holding meetings in the town of Barvas, less than a quarter mile from the church where the Hebrides revival broke out in 1949.

After the first evening meeting, I had the honor of meeting a woman named Christine. She had been sent to the island of Lewis as an intercessor from England. She would walk the beach and her prayers were shaking the island as God was moving powerfully through her intercession. Some things happened and the enemy got in and brought a man into her life that caused her to shut down her intercessory gift completely for four years. This is where she was at on that first night. Here is the rest of the story in her own words:

So this was really where I was at the end of July when you visited Lewis. Dave had spoken to me on the Sunday morning and told me about the meetings and all of a sudden I was desperate to be there. Desperate and scared witless!!

The first evening I was an embarrassed, ashamed, unspiritual, pathetic useless feeble no good Christian hiding behind a smile! The Lord just took me apart, bit by bit by bit - that's the only way I can describe it, and I am so very, very grateful to Him and to you for putting those bits back together at the end of the evening and leaving me to drive home quite literally shaking with hope.

By the end of the third evening I knew exactly where I had to go back to pray the justice, restoration, restitution prayer, but I was going away on holiday the following day so it had to wait for a fortnight!

At the first opportunity when I got back, I drove over to the area I used to live and visited every single place where I'd had contact with his man. I felt it would be wrong to dwell on it in my mind or let it become any sort of nostalgia trip, so I didn't spend long in any one place - just kind of prayed and left, then, in the spirit gathered it all up in a big bundle and headed for my praying beach where I hit it all properly!

I don't quite know what I expected to happen. I think often we hear about other peoples' experiences and expect God to follow the same pattern, then get disappointed when He doesn't. I came away from the beach wondering exactly what had taken place - there'd been no great experience, no flashing lights. If I'm honest, I only knew He'd done something because He'd said He would - that was all.

But ....How awesome have these last 2 months been?!!!!!!! I doubt I can put it into words properly!

One of the first things the enemy had nicked off me those years ago was the intimacy with God as Father - that is soooo being restored. The other big one was being able to intercede without fear; he stole that one big style. But wow, how much is that changing and changing and changing.

I have never known anything like this - there's so much clarity, so much purpose, I'm just gobsmacked. (A British term for astounded) He's showing me what to pray, giving me the words, showing me stuff that's happening spiritually like I'd never have dreamed of. I'm just bursting with it all (and the grammar's going out the window!)

*Thank you **so much** for coming up to Lewis and the teaching you brought. It has quite literally turned me around.*

Hugs,
Christine

What God did in Christine's life was so dramatic that when she heard that we were doing our first official Burning Heart's School of Intercession in Glasgow some months later, she couldn't wait to travel three hours on a ferry and drive 4 1/2 hours to get to Glasgow to join us. Not only that, but over the next year she traveled to Glasgow to assist us two more times in the school. She has been a great blessing to the ministry. Moving to Scotland to see God transform one life like Christine's makes it worth everything.

One of the most dramatic JRR testimonies has to do with my own kids. About a year after I received this revelation, Darla and I returned to Oregon with three of our daughters. We felt we were to take a day and just let the Holy Spirit lead them to where they were to pray JRR. We went to many places that were rather dramatic. One place was the hospital where my oldest daughter Erin was born, before spending the first two weeks of her life in a neonatal intensive care unit. She was born with Double Strep Pneumonia and was given only a 5% chance to live. God intervened and completely healed her. You could feel the spirit of death in the place and then, all of a sudden the atmosphere changed and she began to get better. We went back to the very place and prayed JRR for what the enemy tried to do.

Another place we went was a church where all of us, as a family, had gone through a very difficult time. As we pulled into the parking lot, the three girls began to panic. They said, "Mom and Dad, we don't want to be here." We encouraged them to just stay for a few minutes and they agreed. We sat in the van and prayed the prayer out with much emotion and many tears. While we were praying a woman came and asked us if we needed something. She was the pastor's wife of the church that was currently using the building. We told her who we were and that we also used to live in the house on the church grounds. She asked us if we would like to look around. As we looked around the grounds and went into the sanctuary, we saw the countenances of our daughters change in front of our very eyes.

Even though they were in their late teens and early 20s at the time, they begin to laugh and play like little girls. They would say to each other, "Remember when we did this and had this great time." We could feel the presence of the Lord in the place and it was apparent that God was doing something. It was as if all the bad memories had been washed away and they were only remembering the good times that they had in that place. They were being overwhelmed with the emotion of good memories of things that had happened there. God did a tremendous healing in our girls on that day. Thank you, Jesus.

Final Thought - The message of praying for justice, restoration and restitution has been something that God has been using powerfully around the world. Although many people pray for themselves and their families, it is also a powerful tool in intercession. Praying for families, the lost, cities and nations where the enemy has been at work is what makes JRR so needed in the realms of intercession. I encourage you to make it a regular part of your personal and corporate intercession times. God also wants you personally to be fully equipped for all He is calling you to. Do not hesitate to pray JRR over yourself and your loved ones. God has a great desire to move in your life and situation.

Chapter 7

THE PHENOMENON OF BREAKTHROUGH

An Overused Word

I have always been one for shying away from buzzwords and overused expressions that come through the body of Christ. Sometimes the use of such words is because it is the "cutting-edge" (another example) thing to do. I believe the use of the word "breakthrough" is like that. It seems like everyone is talking about it. In this case however, I believe breakthrough isn't just a fad or buzzword, it is because it's something that God is declaring and releasing to His people in this hour. Let's look at the DNA of this phenomenon we call "breakthrough."

Breakthrough Defined

Once again, I like to get a grasp upon definitions to get wisdom, revelation and understanding about the depth of meaning and the applicability of the word. In the dictionary breakthrough is defined as:

1. A military movement or advance all the way through and beyond an enemy's front-line defense.

2. An act or instance of removing or surpassing an obstruction or restriction; the overcoming of a stalemate: The president reported a breakthrough in the treaty negotiations.

3. Any significant or sudden advance, development, achievement, or increase, as in scientific knowledge or

diplomacy that removes a barrier to progress: The jet engine was a major breakthrough in air transport. (Dictionary.com)

Breakthrough Illustrations

Along with the definitions, here are some great illustrations that will allow us a bigger picture of how God breaking through in a situation is brought forth.

- **A Breakthrough of Water**

The main idea for breakthrough in scripture comes from the breakthrough of water that David used as an illustration of God giving him a tremendous victory over his enemies.

> *"So David went to Baal Perazim, (which **means** "processor of the breaches") and David defeated them there; and he said, 'The LORD has broken through my enemies before me, like a* **breakthrough of water.'** *"* (2 Samuel 5:20)

> *"So David went to Baal-Perazim and defeated the Philistines there. 'The LORD did it!' David exclaimed. 'He burst through my enemies like a raging flood!' So he named that place Baal-perazim."* (which means **"the Lord who bursts through**.) (NLT)

This is a great illustration because the power of moving water is one of the greatest forces in nature. Whether it is a raging flood or tsunami, it can be overwhelmingly devastating to anything in its path. When breakthrough comes, everything that man and the enemy have erected to keep God out of a situation is completely overwhelmed. It is like in the story of Israel being chased by the pharaoh's army. The enemy is swept away as God releases great victory for His people. The breakthrough of water is like a crack in a dam that continues to grow wider and wider.

- **A Troop and a Wall**

The next illustration of breakthrough is from 2 Samuel 22:30. *"For by you I have **run through a troop***: *by my God have **I leaped over a wall**."* When we believe for breakthrough, let's make sure that we are not placing limits on God, who is able to do the impossible. We need to remember that we serve, not only the God of this present world, but also the God of the universe. He is a God who created and is maintaining 400 billion stars in our Milky Way galaxy alone. The estimated number of stars in the universe is 300,000,000,000,000,000,000,000,000, or 300 sextillions. The interesting thing is that God has a name for every last one of them. (Psalm 147:4)

- **Breaking through City Gates**

Another picture of breakthrough is when a walled city is under siege and the opposing army is breaking the gates down with a battering ram. A battering ram is thrust forward time after time until ultimately the gates burst open. The importunity of intercession can be likened to constant and continual calling out to God until the point when the answer comes. In days gone by, this was known as "praying through." Faith and perseverance are central ingredients in intercession that brings breakthrough.

Faith and Perseverance

There are many exhortations in scripture about not quitting and not giving up. Galatians 6:9 says, *"Let us not grow weary while doing good, for in due season we shall reap if we do not lose heart."*

This is what Jesus was communicating as he told the parable of the persistent widow in Luke 18:

*"Then He spoke a parable to them, that men always ought to **pray and not lose heart**, saying, 'There was in a certain city a judge who did not fear God nor regard man. Now there was a widow in that city; and she came to him, saying, 'Get justice for me from my adversary.' And he would not for a while; but afterward he said within himself, 'Though I do not fear God nor regard man, yet because this widow troubles me I will avenge her, lest by her **continual coming** she weary me.' Then the Lord said, 'Hear what the unjust judge said. And shall God not avenge His own elect who cry out day and night to Him, though He bears long with them? I tell you that He will avenge them speedily. Nevertheless, when the Son of Man comes, will He really find faith on the earth?'"*

I had the privilege of hearing Stephen Venable from International House of Prayer in Kansas City teach about these verses. He said that perseverance in prayer is like someone with a pick assaulting a dam. The person with the pick doesn't randomly hit all over the dam, but instead hits repeatedly on one spot. It is the labor of persistent, continual, persevering that brings breakthrough. With repeated blows eventually a crack appears, and then comes the full release.

Mountain Climb - Refusing to Give Up

When I was a young man I went mountain climbing with some friends of mine. We climbed a 10,000-foot mountain in Oregon called, the Middle Sister. We left our base camp at 7,000 feet and began to climb over lava rock and snow banks to steadily make our way towards the summit. As we went along it became very steep and we were buffeted by a bitterly cold wind. The conditions became so severe that one of the two friends I was with said, "I can't do this anymore. I'm going back." He then turned back and headed to base camp.

The other friend that I was with had a very deep and intimate relationship with Jesus. He looked at me and said, "Let's pray." We asked God what to do and then paused for a moment of silence. He then looked me in the eye with a determined gaze and said, "The Lord says He is with us. Let's go." From where we were standing we could not tell, but we were less than five minutes from the summit. The view was spectacular and we could feel God's presence as we were shouting and singing His praises on the mountaintop.

When we returned to base camp we told our other friend what he had missed and that he was almost there. He missed out because he gave up too soon. Oftentimes when we are praying for breakthrough, it is most difficult just before the answer comes. If you will talk to any woman who has delivered a baby, they will tell you that when it gets unbearable the baby is almost here. Let's not give up because we could be just moments from the point of breakthrough.

"When you are tempted to give up, your breakthrough is probably just around the corner." (Joyce Meyer)

The Bowls in Heaven

There are times, when we most want to quit, that we are at the threshold of our breakthrough. Some would say, "We have been praying for years and the change has not come." In the book of Revelations, the 24 elders are given stewardship of something very important. They have in their possession golden bowls full of incense. *"Now when He had taken the scroll, the four living creatures and the twenty-four elders fell down before the Lamb, each having a harp, and golden bowls full of incense, which are the **prayers of the saints**."* (Revelations 5:8)

Could it be that there is a connection between the golden bowls of incense and the pouring out of the Spirit talked about in Joel and the Book of Acts? Could it be that our intercession is directly linked to God pouring out His Spirit in a powerful way? *"But this is what was spoken by the prophet Joel: And it shall come to pass in the last days, says God, That I will pour out of My Spirit on all flesh; Your sons and your daughters shall prophesy, Your young men shall see visions, Your old men shall dream dreams."* (Acts 2:16-17)

Speaking of visions, I had one that might help illustrate what I am talking about. In the vision, I was in heaven with Jesus standing on the rim of a golden bowl that was miles across. The top of the rim was about 12 feet wide. Inside the bowl was a substance that was glowing and moving. I looked at Jesus and asked Him what was in the bowl. He said, "That is My glory." Then He leaned towards me with one eyebrow raised and said with a commanding voice, "I am going to pour this thing out and no one can stop Me."

When God makes up his mind about something there is no one, including Satan, that can oppose Him. This is when the Holy Spirit, the most powerful force in the universe, is released and poured out, and all opposition is defused, defeated and obliterated.

As we fill the bowls in heaven with our prayers there has to come a tipping point. Could it be that the intercession that we offer this day is that which brings the outpouring? It is that which brings the answers to real situations, even impossible situations. Could it be that the tide will turn, the captives will be set free and all that we have dreamed or imagined would be realized?

Prophetic Declaration and Breakthrough

I believe God wants to add to our intercession for breakthrough another element called **prophetic declaration.** The Word says in Psalms 107:2 *"Let the redeemed of the LORD say so."* I believe another way you can say this verse is that, "the redeemed of the Lord **have a say so**." The Lord showed me a picture one time of what prophetic declaration is like. Have you ever seen on the National Geographic Channel those ships in the Arctic that break through solid ice? These ships have a double hull which allows them to rise up on the ice and breakthrough it because of the massive weight of the ship. Prophetic declaration is like the bow of that icebreaking ship. The Word of God, with the weight of God's authority behind it, is released through prophetic declaration and the change comes. If prophetic declaration is like a bow of an icebreaking ship, then intercession is the engine running that ship. The equation is: prophetic declaration + intercession = breakthrough.

This quote from Bill Johnson puts it in perspective;

> *"It is how the economy of heaven works, word is*
> *released and power comes. It's as though you make a*
> *decree and when you do, you put a mark somewhere*
> *and that mark invites God to come. The invitation of*
> *God is the boldness of a declared word."*
> *(From the sermon "The Gospel")*

Areas Needing Breakthrough

There are countless numbers of people, places and situations that need breakthrough. There are so many things that we give serious intercessory prayer time to. This is one of the reasons that, in the kingdom, we need to adopt an "all hands on deck" philosophy when it comes to prayer. We could easily become discouraged by the vast number of things that need prayer. We don't need to be discouraged, we just need to hear the Holy Spirit on what He wants us specifically to pray for. Here are just a few areas that we need to pray for breakthrough in:

- **Justice Issues and Societal Change**

The reason God is concerned about justice issues is because He is deeply moved about those who are suffering the effects of injustice. God's heart can be clearly seen in Isaiah 1:17. *"Learn to do good; Seek justice, Rebuke the oppressor; Defend the fatherless, Plead for the widow."*

Such issues as abortion, human trafficking and poverty must continually be brought before the throne and prayed over. We need breakthrough in these areas and all other justice issues. Of all the avenues of change out there, intercession is the one that has the most potential for breakthrough. There are many testimonies of God working miraculously in the midst of injustice. Intercession is the key to make that possible.

In Luke 4:17-19 Jesus declared Himself as the answer for injustice. *"And He was handed the book of the prophet Isaiah. And when He had opened the book, He found the place where it was written: 'The Spirit of the LORD is upon Me, Because He has anointed Me To preach the gospel to the poor; He has sent Me to heal the brokenhearted, To proclaim liberty to the captives And recovery of sight to the blind, To set at liberty those who are oppressed; To proclaim the acceptable year of the LORD.'"*

Like I said before, God wants to bring real answers to real people, places and situations. He wants to bring change into the society we live in. Societal change should be one of the focuses of our intercession and something we are continually calling upon God for. We do not need to throw our hands in the air and say there is no hope. Jesus is the hope of this world.

Let me give you a few stories of societal change. One is very specific and the other more general. This first story I heard directly from the person who was involved. I am a big believer in accuracy and not embellishing facts and storytelling.

> o My wife and I lived as missionaries in Scotland from 2008 to 2011. We were getting ready to travel to Shetland (The Shetland Islands) to hold a school of intercession and do on-site prayer. I was talking

to a friend of mine named Bert McKaig, who himself is a mighty man of prayer. He said he had been to Shetland a number of years previously and asked if we were going to pray at a fishing town called Scalloway. I told him that we were and he told me a story. He said that when they were in Scalloway they ask the local leaders what the town needed prayer for. They told him that they needed prayer for the fishing industry in Scalloway. The fishing was so bad that many were losing their livelihood in the town. The local economy was being devastated. The group gathered and earnestly prayed for God to do something miraculous about the fishing industry of Scalloway, Shetland.

Then Bert told me that, several years later, he was sitting in the Scottish Parliament when a man got up to give a report on the fishing industry in Scotland. The man said this, "The fishing industry in Scotland has seen an overall increase of 1% everywhere except one place. That one place is Scalloway, Shetland. There has been a 12% increase in the fishing industry in Scalloway." Now that is societal change. Not often do you get to hear the dramatic answer to the intercession that you personally gave. The Lord had arranged for this brother to hear the powerful results of the intercession on that day.

- o Another story of societal change also happened in Scotland. We had joined with many other individuals and ministries to pray for the nation of

Scotland and especially the city of Glasgow. Glasgow is one of the worst cities in Europe for violence, crime, drug use and suicide. In May of 2011 we were given an article from a secular newspaper. The title of the article said, **"VIOLENT CRIME AMONG YOUTH DROPS 31% SINCE 2008".** Wow that is amazing. Now we are not taking credit for this but, we were able to play a part in God bringing a tremendous answer to the city of Glasgow.

- **Financial Breakthrough**

Another area that needs much intercession for breakthrough is the area of finances and provision. Scripture is clear in declaring God's heart towards His people in the area of money. *"And my God shall supply all your need according to His riches in glory by Christ Jesus."* (Ephesians 4:19)

Money is also one of the main components in accomplishing kingdom work. That being the case, it stands to reason that the enemy will oppose the release of finances and provision to God's people. In natural warfare one of the ways to stop an enemy is to set up a blockade. Here is a definition of a blockade:

*A **blockade** is an effort to cut off food, supplies, war material or communications from a particular area by force, either in part or totally.* (Wikipedia)

One of the ways the enemy tries to stop the kingdom from advancing is to cut all the supply lines. The enemy works overtime to convince Christians not to obey God's Word and give liberally. This is why, in the Western world, there is only about 20% of the believers that give anything to God's work. The enemy comes in with fear, mistrust and unbelief in an attempt to sideline believers from doing their part in facilitating God's work going forth.

Then if you add a recession to the mix, it even gets worse. Some people withhold even more when times get tough. In praying for provision and finances, we must ask God to remove the withholding spirit from His people and replace it with a spirit of trust and faith. God's desire is to show Himself even that much stronger in a time of recession. We must see every incident of lack as an opportunity for God's supernatural, miraculous providing power. Here are some synonyms for recession: Bad Times, Bankruptcy, Big Trouble, Bottom-Out, Bust, Collapse, Decline, Deflation, Depression, Downturn, Hard Times, Inflation, Rainy Days, Shakeout, Slide, Slump, Stagnation, Unemployment. It sounds pretty bad, doesn't it? We must not come under, especially in our prayers, the negative, unbelieving spirit of this world. Jesus said in John 16:33, *"These things I have spoken to you, that in Me you may have peace. In the world you will have tribulation; but be of good cheer, I have overcome the world."*

We need to pray for the release of money for kingdom work and then do our part by actually giving. This applies to praying for and giving to individual believers, churches, ministries, prayer and outreach projects, and of course missions. As we pray for the release of kingdom finances, it is very important that we align ourselves with God and his principles of finance and not primarily be influenced by the world's perspective. We need to understand that God doesn't do math, quite like we do. For example, Jesus said give and it shall be given onto you. God wants His people to operate in increase, favor and blessing.

An Invitation to Increase, Favor and Blessing

*"May the LORD **give you increase** more and more,*
you and your children." (Psalms 115:14)

God has given us an invitation to live a life of increase. Now does this mean we will never lack or we will never be in want? Not likely. However, those times of lack should be the occasional, not that which defines our life. Overall, God's desire is for us to increase, not just financially, but in every area of life.

The word increase is defined as: *To Become Greater Or More In Size, Quantity, Number, Degree, Value, Intensity, Power, Authority, Reputation, Wealth; To Grow; To Augment; To Advance; - Opposed To Decrease.* (Webster's) The Hebrew word is *yaw-saf'* which is: *to add or augment, **increase more and more**.* The Greek word is *pleonazo* which is: *to make or be more, that is, increase; by extension,* ***to superabound***: *- abound, abundant, make to increase, have over.* (Strongs)

*"For You, O LORD, will bless the righteous; With **favor***
You will surround him as with a shield." (Psalms 5:12)

The word favor is defined as: *Kind regard; kindness; countenance; propitious aspect; friendly disposition.* (Webster's) The Hebrew words are *ratson ratson* which is: *delight, acceptable delight, desire, favor, good pleasure.* (Strong's) The Greek word is *Charis*, which is: *graciousness.* (Vine's) God wants His people to be those who walk in His favor. Let us intercede to this end.

> *"Let the peoples praise You, O God; Let all the peoples praise You. Then the earth shall yield her **increase**; God, our own **God, shall bless us. God shall bless us,** and all the ends of the earth shall fear Him."* (Psalms 67:5-6)

> *"The blessing of the LORD makes one rich, And He adds no sorrow with it."* (Proverbs 10:22)

The Hebrew word for blessing is *berakah* which is: *benediction, prosperity.* (Strong's) It is still a very legitimate prayer to ask God to bless someone. We should ask God not only to make them happy, but to empower them to succeed, grow and be transformed into the likeness of Jesus. We need to intercede for them to be drawn into the blessing of relationship with God.

Positioned for Increase

As we are praying for increase, it is very important that we understand that God deeply loves people and wants to bless them. I remember once I was praying about some provision to go to the mission field. In my prayer, I slipped into a bit of judgment about people not giving. I said, "Lord we have Christians going on cruises instead of giving to world missions." Then He said, "But what if I want them to go on a cruise?" Ouch. I quickly repented for my bad attitude. Here is a verse that demonstrates that God not only desperately wants to move in people's lives, but that He is well able to do so. The verse is Ephesians 3:20. *"Now to Him who is able to do **exceedingly abundantly above** all that we ask or think, according to **the power** that works in us."*

The two words: *exceedingly abundantly* come together to make one Greek word *huper* which means *over*. I was stunned to discover that the word *above* is also the Greek word *huper*, which means *over*. (Strong's) I believe God, by bringing a double emphasis, is trying to make a point here. It's like the verse is saying, *"Now to Him who is able to do **over, over (or huper, huper)** all that we ask or think, according to the power that works in us."*

God wants us to get the idea that He strongly desires and is well able to do what is even beyond our most dramatic expectations in people's lives. He wants to move in such a way that people actually are pinching themselves, saying, "I had no idea that it was going to be this good." We have yet to scratch the surface on the revelation of the goodness of God. It is something that we will be exploring for eternity.

"Now to Him who is able to [carry out His purpose and] do superabundantly more than all that we dare ask or think [infinitely beyond our greatest prayers, hopes, or dreams], according to His power that is at work within us." (AMP)

We must pray for God to release, and for people to really seek, a spirit of liberality.

I had the privilege of hearing Pastor Frank Damazio speak on this subject. He said, *"Courageous generosity is an attitude that confronts adversity. The attitude that confronts adversity is the spirit of liberality, open handed generosity, unselfish faith-filled giving. Don't give up on the favor of God in your life. Sow a seed in someone else's field."*

"There is one who scatters, yet increases more; And there is one who withholds more than is right, But it leads to poverty."
(Proverbs 11:24)

Breakthrough in Relationships

"There are "friends" who destroy each other, but a real friend sticks closer than a brother." (Proverbs 18:24 NLT)

To God, relationships are a big deal. Not only are they worth working on, they are worth praying for. There are many relationships that we need breakthrough in. Whether it is husband-and-wife, parent and child, siblings or friends, we need God to move in relationships.

I believe the first place we need to start is praying for our own families. Each one of us has an intercessory assignment from the Lord to pray for family members. Fathers and mothers are to pray for their children. Spouses are to pray for each other. There are many other family members that need to be prayed for, especially if that family member is not walking with God. In any person's life, what they need the most, no matter what their situation, is a relationship with Jesus. Here are some ways to pray for loved ones who are not a walking with God:

- **The Undeniable Encounter**

One way to pray is for them to have a face-to-face, road to Damascus, burning bush encounter with the Lord. This is called an **undeniable encounter**. It is God and them coming together to such a degree that it cannot be explained away. Pray that God would give them such an experience that they will be forever changed. The Bible is full of people who encountered God and it changed the course of their life for the rest of their life. If it happened then, why can't we believe for it today? Our prayers release the Holy Spirit to work on them.

- **Divine Encounters with True Christ Followers**

We can also pray that they will have divine encounters with real followers of Jesus. Sometimes the problem is that they have encountered those who have misrepresented God to them. These well-meaning Christians came across as judgmental, without love, harsh, and, ultimately, give that person a sense of rejection. Pray that they meet and are impacted by the Spirit of Christ in people who are truly demonstrating God's love and properly representing Jesus.

- **Prayer Strategy**

I once heard a story of a mother who was very burdened for her backslidden son. He had moved back home, but wanted nothing to do with Jesus. She asked the Lord how to pray for him. The Lord told her that while he was at work she was to go lay on his bed face down and intercede for him. She had been doing this for a good while when, one day, she came home to see her son's car in the driveway. He was home early from work so she went in to look for him. She could not find him in the house. Then she opened the garage door to see him lying face down, weeping, repenting and giving his life back to Jesus. Sometimes we just need to ask, "Lord what is the strategy" We need to believe that God is just getting started to work in their lives.

> *"Being confident of this very thing, that He who has **begun a good work** in you (them) will **complete it** until the day of Jesus Christ."* (Philippians 1:6)

There are many other areas we need to believe God for breakthrough in. Let's take the time to cover each one in prayer and see Him move powerfully.

Manifested Breakthrough

Now I'd like to share with you what I believe to be one of the most powerful aspects of the nature of breakthrough. It is what I call **"Manifested Breakthrough." Manifested breakthrough is not just God breaking into a situation from one direction, but it is God placing himself in the very center of what needs to change and then manifesting his power, glory and presence 360° X 360°. It truly is, "If God is for us, who can be against us."**

The word breakthrough comes from the Hebrew word *perets* which means: *to break out.* In the areas that we believe God for breakthrough in, we should also believe Him to break out from the very center of the situation. Zephaniah 3:17 declares *"the Lord thy God **in the midst** of you is **mighty**."* In this verse the word **midst** is the word *qereb* (key-reb) which means *the nearest part*, that is, *the **centre***. The word **mighty** is the word *gibbor* (gib-bor) which means *a **powerful warrior** or **champion***. (Strong's)

The Lord wants to come as a powerful warrior champion to show Himself strong in the midst of all hindrances, obstacles and blockades that the enemy has erected to stop the flow of God's purposes.

Just like in the epicenter of a nuclear bomb or the flashpoint of a volcano, resistance in every direction is obliterated. God's desire is to bring manifested breakthrough.

Biblical Examples

- **The Battle of Jericho**

The victory at Jericho was not the result of an advancing army breaking into the gates of the city. It was as God's people obeyed and followed His strategy that breakthrough came and the victory was won. Jericho had two walls, an inner and outer, with a combined thickness of 18 feet. I'm sure that the inhabitants of Jericho never imagined that these walls would be breached, let alone be destroyed altogether in a moment of time. Our God is well able to bring breakthrough in the midst of impossible situations.

- **The Manifested Power of the Holy Spirit**

The Holy Spirit, the most powerful force in the universe, is very active on Planet Earth today. We often do not think of His power as being the exact same power that raised Jesus from the dead. The declaration of Romans 8:11 is this; *"But if the Spirit of Him* *who **raised Jesus** from the dead dwells in you, He who raised Christ from the dead will also **give life** to your mortal bodies through His Spirit who dwells in you."* We need to believe God and ask him for the release of Holy Spirit power, the power of the resurrection in our lives.

Scripture also says that the anointing breaks the yoke. Many believers these days are walking around with heavy yokes of everything from religious expectations to orphaned thinking and condemnation. God's desire is to manifest breakthrough to obliterate yolks by the anointing. (Isaiah 10:27)

- **Jesus Calming the Sea**

There are times that the manifestation of breakthrough is going to come with the release of great peace into a situation. In Mark 4, Jesus stood in the **midst** of a storm that the disciples thought was life threatening. In the midst of that storm, He declared, "**Peace, be still**." It's interesting that the response of the storm was not to just ease up a bit, but scripture says "the wind ceased, and there was **a great calm**." I believe God wants to bring great calm in the many storms of life that we face. Even if the circumstances of that storm do not change immediately, we can still receive "a great calm" deep inside our hearts.

**Breakthrough starts within us first, then
travels outward to our circumstances.**
"That He would grant you, according to the riches of His glory, to be strengthened with might through His Spirit in the inner man."
(Ephesians 3:16)

"Breakthrough is not when you have all the finances you need. Breakthrough is when you are not afraid." (Kirk Bennett) There are many other examples of manifested breakthrough in scripture. It seems that God has always been about winning great victories for and through His people.

Final Thought – As we look forward, I believe in the days ahead we are not only going to see a marked increase in the release of signs, wonders and miracles, but also manifested breakthrough in the sudden release of God's power in the impossible situations that need to change in the earth. Let's pray for this, let's believe for this and let's contend for this.

Chapter 8

ONSITE STRATEGIC INTERCESSION

Now we are going to shift to a specific application of intercessory prayer. I believe intercession is to be offensive in the sense that we are to not just pray in our homes and churches, but invade enemy territory and release the power and presence of God on the very ground the enemy has taken. As we go and place our feet in the places God shows us, we will be reclaiming the land, as well as seeing it healed from defilement. I believe this is one of the most powerful means that we can make a difference in intercession. When we pray onsite, we want to be effective, but we also want to be safe. In this type of prayer there are almost as many things not to do as there are to do. Let's look at the whole idea of *Onsite Strategic Intercession*.

Why Go Onsite?

When we talk about Onsite Strategic Intercession, it is really just a fancy term for prayer walking. Except for the fact that it is not as much about the walking as it is about going somewhere to pray and get our feet on the land. Usually the places we go have some sort of a historical, social or spiritual significance.

Praying onsite is extremely thrilling and exciting. In my opinion, the only thing that rivals it in excitement would be power evangelism on the streets. However, even though it is exciting, many would ask the question, "Is it not enough for us to pray within the safe, protective walls of our churches and homes? Do we really need to 'get out there' so to speak? Let's look at some of the reasons why it is important to do intercession onsite.

Increased Anointing As We Carry His Presence

*"And the LORD said to Abram, after Lot had separated from him, 'Lift your eyes now and look from the place where you are … Arise, **walk in the land** through its length and its width, for I give it to you.' "* (Genesis 13:14-17)

*"Every place that the sole of your **foot will tread** upon I have given you, as I said to Moses."* (Joshua 1:3)

One of the ways we invade enemy territory is by carrying the presence of the King with us everywhere we go. We are to be a people of His presence that are continually confronting and changing the negative atmosphere around us. This especially applies as we go places to pray. We can bring His presence that will leave a lasting effect. When David stepped forward in a different spirit and defeated the giant, it transformed the atmosphere that was hovering over the armies of Israel. Instead of being overwhelmed by fear, defeat and doubt, they were impacted by a new atmosphere of courage, faith and victory. As we walk the land, we bring the presence of our amazing victorious King and things begin to change.

Healing the Land

One of the main focuses for Onsite Strategic Intercession is to bring healing to the land of the place we are praying. One might say, "What does the land have to do with anything?" Here is what the Word says in 2 Chronicles 7:14, *"If My people who are called by My name will humble themselves, and pray and seek My face,* *and turn from their wicked ways, then I will hear from heaven, and will forgive their sin and **heal their land**."* Yes those words, 'heal their land' have been there all this time. Usually this verse deals with the humbling, the praying and the turning, but it is all for the final conclusion which is to **heal the land**. There is a definite connection in the spiritual realm between the land and what goes on with the people of the land. This concept is very accepted by most cultures except for the western world. I know this may sound a bit strange but please hear me out. As God heals the land, the enemy will be defeated and God will begin to move in the people of the land.

Land Defilement

When we talk about the need for healing in the land, what we are referring to is land defilement issues. The word defile means *make dirty; spoil or pollute, desecrate*. As the land is healed, there is an opening of the spiritual atmosphere that makes a way for God to move.

Many of us have heard of places where there is what we refer to as, "an open heaven." The Celtic Apostles referred to these geographic sites as "thin places." That is because it seemed as if the veil between heaven and earth was much thinner there. In those places it is very easy to be impacted by the presence and power of God. On the other hand, there are places that are just the opposite.

Have you ever been to a place of evil where you could actually feel the negative spiritual atmosphere? When you were there you had to pit in your stomach and possibly became physically ill because of the evil atmosphere. That is a place that is defiled and is operating under a demonic curse. Because of the sin of the people of the land, the land is defiled and it brings about the opposite of an open heaven which is an opening to hell. **Defiled land equals a closed heaven and an opening to hell.** The sins of the people give the enemy **legal right** to operate there.

I first became aware of this spiritual reality in 1998. I was still very new in my journey as an intercessor. I went with a team to Ayutthaya, Thailand to intercede in preparation for a missionary planting a church there. We were going around to various sites of historical and spiritual significance. One of the places we went was an ancient palace site. Ayutthaya was the former capital of the nation of Siam, now Thailand. At this palace site, 700 years previous, the king was having a bad day and had 3000 of his own people killed. That sin had left a stain of defilement on the land. We went to the very site where this atrocity took place. As we were praying and repenting, I had a vision. At this point I had not heard of anything like what I was seeing. I saw a vision of a large hole in the ground. Out of this hole were demons coming back and forth like from a beehive in the ground. This hole was probably 30 to 40 feet across.

I was reminded of John 1:51 where Jesus referred to an open heaven, where angels were ascending and descending. Except this was the exact opposite. As we were praying I saw the ground around the hole begin to tremble. Then, in an instant of time, the hole came together and was violently closed, crushing demons in the collapsed vortex. I was so excited to share with the team the vision I saw. I was amazed that a few people from

America and a missionary to Thailand could pray and God would close an access point to hell that had been open for over 700 years. When land is defiled it gives the enemy legal right to bring the substance of hell and spew it on the earth. Things were changing and shifting over Thailand.

What Causes Land Defilement

There are four primary causes for land defilement. They are:

- Innocent bloodshed
- Broken covenants
- Idolatry
- Immorality.

*"Hear the word of the LORD, You children of Israel, For the LORD brings a charge against the inhabitants of **the land**: "There is no truth or mercy or knowledge of God in **the land**. By **swearing and lying, killing and stealing** and **committing adultery**, they break all restraint, **with bloodshed** upon bloodshed. Therefore, **the land will mourn**."* (Hosea 4:1-4)

*"Son of man, when the house of Israel dwelt in their **own land, they defiled it** by their own ways and deeds; to Me their way was like the uncleanness of a woman in her customary impurity."* (Ezekiel 36:17)

"The land is defiled when man refuses to worship the one true Creator God and turns to other idolatrous practices, such as: worshipping riches, bloodshed, sexual perversions and broken covenants; which are some of the root causes. Defilement of the land

creates legal grounds for the demonic to gain footholds and to attach
to local cultures, including institutional demonic strongholds."
(Lockley C. Bremner, Native American)

Innocent Bloodshed

"And He said, 'What have you done? The voice of your brother's
*blood cries out to Me **from the ground**. So now you are cursed from*
the earth, which has opened its mouth to receive your brother's blood
from your hand.'" (Genesis 4:10-11)

*"So ye shall not **pollute the land** wherein you are: for blood **defiles***
***the land**: and the land cannot be cleansed of the blood that is shed*
therein, but by the blood of him that shed it." (Numbers 35:33)

In any place where there is bloodshed, especially innocent bloodshed, a curse comes on the land. The most obvious example of this, of course, is abortion. But also everything from the murder of an individual, to battlefields where thousands are killed… the blood cries out from the ground.

I heard a story of an intercessor brother who went to Russia and asked the Pastor he was with about a certain hill that he saw. When the pastor asked him why he wanted to know, he said that, in the spiritual realm, he could hear the innocent blood crying from the ground. The pastor, with a stunned look on his face, went on to tell him that on that hill thousands of Christians were martyred by the communists.

Of course the first incident of blood crying from the ground is in the story of Cain and Abel.

"Then the LORD said to Cain, 'Where is Abel your brother?'
He said, 'I do not know. Am I my brother's keeper?' And He
*said, 'What have you done? The voice of your brother's **blood***
cries out to Me from the ground.'" (Genesis 4:9-10)

Broken Covenants

"The earth is also defiled under its inhabitants, because they
have transgressed the laws, Changed the ordinance, broken
the everlasting covenant." (Isaiah 24:5)

Tremendous value is given by God to us following through with
that which we agree to. In Numbers 30:2 this is illustrated. *"If a*
man makes a vow to the LORD, or swears an oath to bind himself by
some agreement, he shall not break his word; he shall do according to
all that proceeds out of his mouth." When covenants, agreements
or treaties, especially by governmental authorities, are broken
the land is defiled.

Idolatry

"On that day a fountain will be opened for the dynasty of
*David and for the people of Jerusalem, **a fountain to cleanse** them*
from all their sins and impurity. And on that day," says the LORD
*of Heaven's Armies, "I will **erase idol worship throughout the***
***land**, so that even the names of the idols will be forgotten. I will*
*remove from the land both the false prophets and the **spirit of***
***impurity** that came with them."* (Zechariah 13:1-2)

Intentional false worship, as well as a dark atmosphere, is that
which brings defilement over the land. The release of the
demonic through false religions, pagan worship, new age,

Freemasonry, etc. happens more often than we might think. If you travel to places like Asia, demonic false worship is not hidden, but it is right there in your face confronting you.

In 2012 I spent a month in the nation of Cambodia. I traveled all over the nation with a Cambodian missionary named Chuck McCaul. I began to notice in many places there were statues and carvings of multi-headed snakes. He said that they were revering a serpent or dragon named Naga. When Buddha received his enlightenment this serpent came and coiled up and had Buddha sit on the coil. Then this serpent, with five heads incorporated in one large cobra like head, hovered over Buddha during the time of enlightenment. Let's see, spiritual being called a serpent or dragon, which is there when a religious leader comes up with a plan to deceive possibly billions of people. I don't think there is any doubt that it is Satan himself we are talking about here. This false worship is defiling the land.

The enemy draws power from false worship. As the spirits entice humans into agreeing with them, they are able to exercise more control in that land.

Immorality
*"For the land is **full of adultery**, and it **lies under a curse**. The **land itself** is in **mourning**."* (Jeremiah 23:10 NLT)

The increase of sexual sin in society today has brought a tremendous curse on the land. Whole cities such as Amsterdam or Bangkok have been given over to prostitution, which has brought a curse. The blight of human trafficking and sex slavery has grown to unimaginable levels and has stained the land across the globe. Then there is pornography, which I heard one guy call the marketing for human trafficking. It is at levels we never could have imagined just a few years ago. Scripture is very clear that sexual sin comes with a price.

*"For by means of a harlot a man is **reduced** to a crust of bread;*
And an adulteress will prey upon his precious life."
(Proverbs 6:26)

Notice the word 'reduced' in this verse. All of sexual sin robs from not only the one partaking of it, but also from the land where they live. Then it is compounded even more when governments and societies embrace sexual activity that is banned by scripture. Our first responsibility is for ourselves. We need to live pure before the Lord. Then we can begin to pray for God to turn the tide of this evil in our land.

Identification Repentance

Once again in 2 Chronicles 7:14, as we turn from our wicked ways, then He will forgive our sin and heal our land. It's not just our sin, but the sin of those we are standing in for. As we step into that place of repentance for those who have gone before, God will begin to heal the land. I've included below some great quotes:

"Why should we be concerned about what our ancestors might have done? This is an important question raised by many who hear of identificational repentance for the first time. The answer derives from the spiritual principle that iniquity passes from

179

generation to generation. One of many biblical texts on the matter comes from the Ten Commandments that Moses received on Sinai: 'I, the Lord, your God, am a jealous God, visiting the iniquity of the fathers on the children to the third and fourth generations...' (Exodus 20:5). Technically speaking, sin can be understood as the initial act while iniquity is the effect that the sin has exercised on subsequent generations."
From '**The Power to Heal the Past' by C. Peter Wagner**

"We are called to live out the Biblical practice of identification repentance, a neglected truth that opens the floodgates of revival and brings healing to the nations."
from '**Healing America's Wounds' by John Dawson**

"Any time we pray for the land to be healed, we should include identification repentance. I came across this great definition. 'Identification repentance is a term referring to a type of prayer which identifies with and confesses before God the corporate sins of one's nation, people, church, or family.' Such sins often stand in the way of revival, and God seems to move with greater blessing and power to advance the gospel and the cause of Christ where the Body of Christ prays this way."
by Gary S. Greig

Owning the Sin

I remember after teaching this in one of our schools of intercession someone came up with this question. "How can we repent for someone else's sin, especially that of a previous generation?" That is a good question. Here are some scriptures that might shed some light:

*"Then I set my face toward the Lord God to make request by prayer and supplications, with fasting, sackcloth, and ashes. And I prayed to the LORD my God, and **made confession**, and said, "O Lord, great and awesome God, who keeps His covenant and mercy with those who love Him, and with those who keep His commandments, **WE** have sinned and committed iniquity, **WE** have done wickedly and rebelled, even by departing from Your precepts and Your judgments. Neither have **WE** heeded Your servants the prophets, who spoke in Your name to our kings and our princes, to our fathers and all the people **OF THE LAND**."* (Daniel 9:3-6)

*"Then those of Israelite lineage separated themselves from all foreigners; and they stood and **confessed their sins** and the **iniquities of their fathers**."* (Nehemiah 9:2)

Standing in proxy for the sins of our generation and the generations previous is the key to not only cleansing the land, but rolling away the reproach of that sin.

Reconciliation Enactments

Reconciliation Enactments are specifically designed to heal riffs and offenses between people groups. The groups could be from nations, cities, tribes or families. It is best to actually go and place your feet on the land where that particular people group live or the offenses which caused the riff took place. This kind of prayer is especially effective with a group of people. Below you will see how a Reconciliation Enactment should be implemented. Here are the primarily elements to a Reconciliation Enactment:

181

- Apology
- Receiving the Apology
- Declare Blessing over the Other Group
- Expressing Love and Forgiveness with Hugs and Handshakes

It's also helpful to have those in the group who are directly connected to one of the two sides of the offense. Ask if they were born there or they are of the bloodline of that particular group. Have the two groups get into lines facing each other. Ask each group to elect a spokesperson for their group.

Have the spokesperson for the first group give an official apology for their part in the offence and bringing division with the other group. Then have the spokesperson from the other group officially receive the apology. Do the same the other way with the other group apologizing and the opposite group receives the apology.

Then have each group speak and pray a blessing on the other group. Have them express their love and forgiveness to each other by coming together with handshakes and hugs.

The first time I was a part of one such reconciliation was in Thailand. We were invited to go with a group of Thai and Burmese pastors to an ancient royal elephant pen. At this place there were life-sized bronze statues depicting the invasion of Thailand by Burma centuries before. It was around 95°f and high humidity with nothing but dirt underneath our feet. As these Burmese pastors began to apologize for the invasion, they got down on their knees while wearing white shirts and slacks and, with many tears, apologized. When it was finished they rose to their feet and all these pastors embraced one another and wept. I was stunned by what I was seeing and was aware that what they were doing was not only important but powerful.

Another powerful reconciliation enactment that we were involved in was in a town called Berwick-upon-Tweed on the English/Scottish border in northeast England. This is a town that had gone back and forth between England and Scotland 14 times.

In 1296 King Edward Longshanks invaded Scotland and his first city of conquest was Berwick-upon-Tweed. He destroyed the town and killed all 8,000 men, women and children residing there. We went to a park near the River Tweed on a hill overlooking the town. We had come from Glasgow with a group of about 15. I asked if any in the group were born in England or had English descent. We had five English and eight Scots lined up across from one another. To represent the Scots, we chose a man named Mark Campbell. Mark is a quintessential Glaswegian with a thick accent. How he came to know the Lord was quite interesting. He had just gotten out of prison for attempted murder and was in his living room getting ready to watch a movie. Then all of a sudden Jesus showed up in his living room. As he stood there transfixed, Jesus said to him, "Mark, I love you. Why are you persecuting me?" Mark said, "I'm sorry, I'm sorry, I'm sorry, I'm sorry!" As the burden of sin was lifted, an incredible joy filled his heart. He ran into the streets to tell people, "It's true, He's alive, He's alive." He is now a radical evangelist and prayer warrior in Scotland.

On the other side, representing the English, a man volunteered that was quite a surprise to us. He was a quiet, meek man named Kevin Winsley. Kevin was born in England but now lives in Scotland.

As we began, Mark filled us in on the history of the invasion. We were awestruck. We started with the English apologizing for the invasion. Kevin was amazing. Under the anointing, this man became an English statesman. He spoke with authority, passion and intentionality. We were all amazed. Mark, representing the Scots, received the apology. Then Mark apologized for all the animosity that the Scots had harbored against the English. The English received the apology.

They then prayed a blessing for each other and ran toward each other and embraced. Many wept as if they were the actual ones involved in what happened 716 years ago. As we were finishing, a dear friend named Tracy McVey spoke up. She was born in Galway, Ireland and wondered if we could say a prayer for the Irish as well. So we all, Scots, English and Americans, gathered around her and prayed for her and blessed the nation of Ireland. God only knows what was accomplished in the spirit realm by that day's event. What an honor to be involved in such an incredible event.

Here are some other reconciliation enactments that I have been a part of:

- Clan Campbell and Clan Macdonald - Glencoe Massacre - Glencoe, Scotland
- Highland Clans Reconciliation – Inverness, Scotland
- Cherokee and Early Americans – Swannanoa, North Carolina
- Adjoining Cities – Eugene/Springfield, Oregon

"Now all things are of God, who has reconciled us to Himself through Jesus Christ, and has given us the ministry of reconciliation, that is, that God was in Christ reconciling the world to Himself, not imputing their trespasses to them, and has committed to us the word of reconciliation." (2 Corinthians 5:18, 19)

Land Rejoicing

*"So shall My word be that goes forth from My mouth; It shall not return to Me void, but it shall accomplish what I please, and it shall prosper in the thing for which I sent it. "For you shall go out with joy, and be led out with peace; The **Mountains and the hills shall break forth into singing before you,** and all the **trees of the field shall clap their hands.**"* (Isaiah 55:11-12)

Once I was praying on top of a hill called Arthur's Seat in Edinburgh, Scotland with a group of men. From that place, we were rededicating the land of Scotland to the Lord. The Lord had directed us to "have communion with the land." As we prayed, we picked up a rock and placed bread and wine on the ground and put the rock over it. As we finished praying, one of the guys named Jeremy Wagaman was overcome by the joy of the Lord. He shouted, "Can you feel it? It is like the land is rejoicing. It is like Isaiah 55 where it says the mountains and hills shall break forth with singing." Then he proceeded to run down the mountain shouting and rejoicing. We all had a strong witness of the Spirit, that what he was saying was really happening. The land was beginning to heal. As we pray onsite God releases his presence with joy, resulting in an open heaven. (Psalms 16:11)

Preparation and Implementation of Onsite Prayer

Here are some steps to take before the time of prayer and as you gather to pray together at the site.

- **Not to be taken lightly - No Attitudes**

Onsite intercession is serious business. We are never to have a cheeky, arrogant attitude about what we are doing.

- **Know the History – Mapping**

It can be a real help to know some of the history of the place you are praying especially if it relates to the four areas of defilement.

- **Combination of Pre-Planning and Holy Spirit Leading**

A combination of prayerful pre-planning and leading of the Holy Spirit during the prayer is best for onsite intercession. There are things that He will show you ahead of time and things that you will become aware of as you are there to pray.

- **Confess Sin**

It is good to take some personal time with the Holy Spirit for each team member to become aware of any area of sin that needs to be confessed. Then declare that the team is covered in the blood of Jesus. It is important to pray with a clean slate so as to give the enemy no advantage.

- **Mantle of Humility**

I believe the mantle of humility to be an actual spiritual garment that we need to wear in any onsite prayer endeavor. Take a moment and ask the team to go through the motions of putting on this garment and embracing humility. I believe this is the undergarment for the armor of God.

- **Armor of God**

Take a moment and have the team put on the armor of God. Once again have them act out actually placing armor on their body. You may want to pray through the list of armor in Ephesians 6.

- **Flow with One in Charge**

It is a good idea to have someone in charge of the team. God works in delegated leadership. That way, if there is any dispute about the direction to go in prayer, the one in charge can be the one to decide. This will also guard the unity of the team.

- **If Attacked, Get Prayer**

Tell the team that if anyone senses that they are being attacked by the enemy (headaches and dizziness, etc.), they should get prayer immediately. Tell them not to wait until the end of the prayer time. We have authority over every demon spirit who tries to personally attack any of our team members. This does not happen very often in an onsite prayer session, but it is good to be aware just in case. Pray a hedge over the team before you go and the likelihood of this happening will be minimized.

Prophetic Acts for Onsite Strategic Intercession

- ### Pouring Out Water

This represents the cleansing and washing of the land and, ultimately, the people of the land through salvation.

"After seven months, teams of men will be appointed to search the land for skeletons to bury, so the land will be made clean again." (Ezekiel 39:14 NLT)

- ### Scattering Salt

This represents the returning of the savor and flavor of the Lord in the land. It also speaks of the salt covenant and is also symbolic of making people thirsty for the living water that Jesus has to offer.

*"Should you not know that the LORD God of Israel gave the **dominion** over Israel to David forever, to him and his sons, by a covenant of salt?"* (2 Chronicles 13:5)

*"And he said, 'Bring me a new bowl, and put **salt** in it.' So they brought it to him. Then he went out to the source of the water, and cast in the **salt** there and said, "Thus says the LORD, 'I have **healed this water**; from it there shall be **no more death or barrenness**."* (2 Kings 2:20, 21)

- **Pouring Out Oil**

This represents the **Anointing of the Holy Spirit** and His power to bring change in the land. You also want to pray that the **Holy Spirit activity** in that geographic area will increase. It is good to declare something like, **"Holy Spirit we honor you in this place."**

"It shall come to pass in that day That his burden will be taken away from your shoulder, and his yoke from your neck, And the yoke will be destroyed because of the anointing oil." (Isaiah 10:27)

Prophetic Acts Implementation

In pouring out the salt, the water and the oil, choose someone from the group and have them pour out the element as they are praying a prayer related to that particular prophetic act. Do these each, one at a time. After they are finished praying, have two or three more from the team pray in relationship to the topic.

Other Prophetic Acts

Here are some other prophetic acts and you might implement during a time of onsite intercession:

- Ringing a Hand Bell - Symbol of a Sweet Sound
- Blowing the Shofar - A Reminder to the Enemy of the Last Trumpet
- Beating Drums - Bring the team into Rhythm
- Build a Spiritual Altar - Calling Back the Good that has been Lost
- Driving Wooden Stakes with Scripture Written on Them
- Releasing the Dance
- Making Declarations and Decrees

- Declaring Scripture

This list of prophetic acts is by no means exclusive. Ask the Lord about other prophetic acts that He may want you to implement during a specific time of prayer.

Other Directives

At the beginning of this session, we talked about being effective, but also being safe. Remember, we are invading enemy territory. There are lines we should not cross in order to remain on solid, safe, scriptural ground. I believe that we do not have to "expect" backlash from the enemy. If we do things right, we will be effective, but also remain safe relating to us, the team we are praying with, our families and our stuff. Here are some points of wisdom that will help us remain safe and effective in *Onsite Strategic Intercession*:

- **Pray in the Opposite Spirit**

If you are praying about something negative, don't focus your prayers on that, but pray and ask God to release the opposite, good thing of what needs to change.

- **Pray For "Them" Not "Us"**

Intercession is always about praying for others. It is helpful to stay away from "we" or "us" and pray for "they" or "them." The only exception is when we are doing identification repentance and repenting on behalf of the people of the land.

- **Pray For (Positive) - Not Against (Negative)**

Keep your prayers positive. Intercession is to pray for God to release the good, which will in turn displace that which is evil, hurtful and destructive.

- **No Rebuking, Binding or Coming Against Directly**

Onsite prayer is not the place to focus on binding and rebuking the enemy directly. We are not to go out and directly confront Satan, principalities and powers or evil in society. When I say evil in society, I am speaking of binding the people that are working to promote that evil. In onsite prayer we do not want to use words such as: we come against, we rebuke, or we take authority over. Especially when praying for cities and nations. We'll be discussing this further in the chapter on The Principles and Protocols of Warfare.

I especially want to emphasize the importance of not rebuking principalities and powers. The model in scripture is Daniel, Chapter 10. Daniel interceded, which was his job, and the angels confronted the Prince of Persia (a principality). We must follow the model of Daniel 10 and do our job, which is intercession.

- **Ending the Prayer Time**

It is always good to pray over the team members and their families before you finish. Declare that there will be no backlash of the enemy and that they will be hidden and protected by the Lord in the secret place of the Most High. (Psalms 91) Then pray a blessing on each one for their willingness to come out and serve the Lord.

It is always good to seal the time of prayer with a worship song that everyone would know.

Final Thought - I believe God wants us to be as equally effective in praying onsite as we are in the prayer closet. As the Holy Spirit leads us into the realms of intercession on the land, we will see God do powerful things to effect change that will be tangible.

Chapter 9
INTERCESSION AND WARFARE – PART I

Defeating the Spirit of Jezebel

A Real Enemy

I n the next two chapters we are going to look at the whole subject of spiritual warfare as it relates to intercession. As I have said before, intercession is a great threat to the kingdom of darkness. In the next chapter we will cover more thoroughly the subject of spiritual warfare. In this chapter, I will be primarily telling a story.

This is the story of how I dealt with a particular Jezebel spirit. The title, "Defeating the Spirit of Jezebel," does not indicate there is only one of this particular type of spirit, but rather is an example of many similar spirits that attack.

Scripture says that our warfare here on earth is not to be waged with our focus being on people, but that our focus must be on the Lord and how He wants to defeat   demonic forces that are attacking mankind. What I am about to share with you is an encounter with just such an entity.   As God has been emphasizing the release of his people into prophetic understanding, there has been an opposition that has come to distract, infiltrate and, if possible, destroy leaders, churches and ministries.   The demonic force we are talking about is most commonly referred to as the Spirit of Jezebel. I believe this is one of the main demonic spirits that comes to oppose, not just intercessors, but intercession by the church. If the enemy can get us defeated and distracted, we will not be praying many prayers that make a difference.

The main reference that gives us insight into that spirit is in Revelations 2:18 -22.

"And to the angel of the church in Thyatira write, these things says the Son of God, who has eyes like a flame of fire, and His feet like fine brass, 'I know your works, love, service, faith, and your patience; and as for your works, the last are more than the first.

Nevertheless, I have a few things against you, because you allow that woman Jezebel, who calls herself a prophetess, to teach and seduce my servants to commit sexual immorality and eat things sacrificed to idols. And I gave her time to repent of her sexual immorality, and she did not repent. Indeed, I will cast her into a sickbed, and those who commit adultery with her into great tribulation, unless they repent of their deeds.'"

What I am bringing forth in this chapter is not so much a teaching about the Spirit of Jezebel, as it is the recounting of an experience I had in January and February of 2008. I might warn you that some of the things I share could be hard or difficult to come to grips with. What we are dealing with is the work of the enemy primarily in believer's lives. The thing we need to be aware of is that, if the Lord reveals something to you about your own life in relationship to Jezebel, just renounce it, repent and give it to God. It might be easy to think of someone else to whom this may apply, but what I encourage you to do is just focus on your own heart before the Lord. We do not want to bring an accusation unjustly against another brother or sister. We really need to be careful in this area.

A Specific Calling

You must understand that the story that I'm about to share with you is connected to my calling as an intercessor and a warrior in the kingdom. It took me 12 years of learning the protocols of intercession and spiritual warfare to be at a place where the Lord could lead me into the realms of warfare like this. It's not that my calling is better than anyone else's, it's just that there has to be understanding in order to deal with the enemy at this level. So I would like to admonish you to have a, "do not try this at home" approach, unless you are ready.

The Journey Begins

The story begins as I was beginning a 40 day fast on January 2nd, 2008 in Asheville North Carolina. During this time, I had been devoting about two to four hours a day to intercession and seeking the Lord. When I pray, I usually get out in the woods and walk the hiking trails. This allows me to focus on the Lord and, more importantly, stay awake. During that time, God began to speak to me about what He was doing in the body of Christ and what he was requiring of us. Though some of these things may seem a bit negative or critical, I believe God wants to bring us to a place where He can truly release the positive blessings of walking with Him. Here are some things that I believe the Lord spoke to me during the first 30 days of the fast.

- **Purity, Holiness, Integrity and Righteousness**

I heard the Lord say, "I want purity, holiness, integrity and righteousness in this season."

"Who may ascend into the hill of the LORD? Or who may stand in His holy place? He who has clean hands and a pure heart, who has not lifted up his soul to an idol, nor sworn deceitfully. He shall receive blessing from the LORD, and righteousness from the God of his salvation." (Psalms 24:3-5)

"Dishonest scales are an abomination to the LORD, but a just weight is His delight. When pride comes, then comes shame; but with the humble is wisdom. The integrity of the upright will guide them, but the perversity of the unfaithful will destroy them." (Proverbs 11:1-3)

Purity is moral cleanness. It is defined as: Free from moral defilement, without spot, not sullied or tarnished, incorrupt, holy.

Holiness is moral purity. It is defined as: The state of being holy, purity or integrity of moral character, freedom from sin, sanctity.

Integrity is moral innocence. It is defined as: The entire, unimpaired state of anything, particularly of the mind, moral soundness or purity, incorruptness, uprightness, honesty. Integrity comprehends the whole moral character.

Righteousness is moral rightness. It is defined as: Purity of heart and rectitude of life, conformity of heart and life to the divine law. (Webster)

- **The Fear of the Lord**

I heard the Lord speak to me about and I experienced "the fear of Lord."

"The Spirit of the LORD shall rest upon Him, The Spirit of wisdom and understanding, The Spirit of counsel and might, The Spirit of knowledge and of the fear of the LORD." (Isaiah 11:2)

"The fear of the LORD is the beginning of knowledge, but fools despise wisdom and instruction." (Proverbs 1:7)

Over the past 40+ years I have been in a lot of meetings, some of which have had a serious atmosphere in them. There have been those times where the fear of the Lord would show up in a meeting and all we would want to do was get on our faces and call out to God. It's like we almost begged the Lord to show us any area of sin in our lives so we could repent of it. There have also been meetings where it was heavy, but it was often caused by a religious spirit or the person leading the meeting bringing guilt and condemnation upon the body. In these days we need to be discerning and respond to the fear of the Lord and not to the fear of man.

- **The Standard of Righteousness**

I heard the phrase, "There is no standard of love without a standard of righteousness."

*"He brought me to the banqueting house and his banner
over me was love."* (Song of Songs 2:4)

*"Righteousness exalts a nation, but sin is a reproach to
any people."* (Proverbs 14:34)

This statement almost sounds like a call to return to legalism. I believe what the Lord is calling for is a standard of righteousness, not legalism (which is a standard of self-righteousness). We need to make sure that the great freedom we have experienced, especially over the last several decades, stays within the moral standards of Scripture, as well as not violating our relationship with Jesus. We need to allow the Holy Spirit to let us know if we have stepped over the line of allowing our liberty to become an occasion for the flesh.

I don't believe the Lord is calling for our return back to outward works and legalism. I believe He is referring to dealing with the issues of a heart. It is making sure our heart and behavior lineup with His character and the directives in the Word.

*"Keep your heart with all diligence, for out of it spring
the issues of life."* (Proverbs 4:23)

*"Therefore gird up the loins of your mind, be sober, and rest
your hope fully upon the grace that is to be brought to you at the
revelation of Jesus Christ; as obedient children, not conforming
yourselves to the former lusts, as in your ignorance; but as He who
called you is holy, you also be holy in all your conduct, because it
is written, "Be holy, for I am holy."* (1 Peter 1:13-16)

God Is Good and That Settles It

Back to the journey... On the morning of January 31st I was sitting in my car at a park by the French Broad River about to start my prayer time. My plans were to hike the "Shut In Trail." This trail was originally built as a hunting trail between the Biltmore Estate and Mount Pisgah in Western North Carolina. Before I got out of the car and began the hike, the Lord wanted me to settle something first. I had been going through a very difficult time and found myself complaining to the Lord. The difficulty was so profound that I began to cry from frustration. I was a bit angry with God. I said, "I told you that I never wanted to be in this position again. I can't believe I am here again." Then a song came on my iPod. It was from a worship leader named Ian Macintosh. The song was called "Always Good." Here's what the lyrics to this song said:

Incline Your ear, You're my one fear God
I need to see You today

It's in Your grace that I'm at peace
You are so faithful God

You are always good God
You are always good

You are always, good God
You are always good

The Lord was asking me over and over, "Do you believe that I'm good?" Finally, while pounding my hands on the steering wheel,

I cried out, "Okay I admit it! You're good, You're good, YOU ARE GOOD!"

An Unexpected Warfare

Once that was settled, I got out of the car and began to hike up the trail towards Mount Pisgah. As I began to pray, something very unusual happened. My mind was bombarded with visions of Christian men who were involved with verbal abuse and domestic violence with their wives. The longer I walked, the more grieved my spirit became. To the point that about 10 minutes into the hike, I began to ask the Lord what was going on. I said, "Lord why am I having these visions? If this is my mind just running on something, please, I beg you, shut it off."

As I hiked up the trail, the visions continued until I was at a point where I had walked about 3 miles. Then all of a sudden it hit me. I said out loud, "It's Jezebel." I remembered that in 1995 (the year that the Lord had called me to give my life for intercession and warfare) I had done a personal study on the spirit of Jezebel. Of all the books I read and tapes I listened to, no one had ever mentioned that Jezebel was the spirit behind domestic violence. The Lord himself showed me that it was. When I came to the realization about the spirit of Jezebel being connected to the visions I was having, I then saw her with my spiritual eyes.

It must be understood that much of the rest of this story is going to involve what we call "seeing in the spirit." There are times when God will allow us to see things spiritually as clearly as we can see things in the natural. It's like God takes over our imagination and allows us to see things on the screen of our mind with detailed clarity. This is what happened on that day. As I looked upon this spirit, the anger of the Lord filled my heart. I knew it was His anger because it didn't feel like the natural anger that I have experienced in the past. Then I said to this spirit as the words flowed from my heart, "You had better get your act together and you had better cover up all your lies because I am coming after you." Typically, I don't immediately address demonic spirits that I see. But somehow this time was different.

The Detaining Angels

As I looked at the spirit, it was in female form and was being held by two angels. As they were holding her, she was extremely angry at me because she was aware that I could see her.

I asked the Lord about who the two angels were, and He spoke to my heart that they were "detaining angels". I had never heard of detaining angels before, but I was sure glad that they were there. They had a hold of this spirit by the arms and it was writhing in anger. I prayed, "Lord would you give these angels strength to hold her." As I did, the scene went from each of the angels gripping her with two hands, to then standing erect, each holding an arm with only one hand. Then one of the angels leaned forward, spoke to me and said with a smile, "We can hold her for days if you need us to."

A New Anointing

I was just about to do warfare with this spirit when the Lord spoke to my heart. He said, "You need to hold on. I am giving you a 36-hour assignment to take this spirit out. For 30 days you have been moving in a priestly ministry of intercession. Now I am switching you to a kingly and prophetic anointing. The kingly anointing is that of Jehu (the king who killed the actual woman, Jezebel) and the prophetic anointing of Elijah who confronted her prophets of Baal. I had a warfare anointing on me that was unlike anything that I had experienced to that date.

Then the Lord began to give me instructions for the next day and a half. You see, I had been a fasting for 30 days and I was weakened physically. Especially with hiking every day, my energy was low. The Lord told me to go home and prepare for this time. He said, "I want you to buy six power bars (peanut butter is my favorite). As I began to head back to the car, I felt led to call my wife Darla, who was with another intercessor friend of ours. I asked them if they would pray about an assignment that the Lord had just given me and that I would be there soon.

As they prayed, Darla immediately heard Ephesians 6:10, *"Finally, my brethren, be strong in the Lord and in the power of His might."* Our friend heard from the Lord Psalm 12, about God rescuing his people. When I arrived, they told me what the Lord had said to them and it was a great confirmation. In warfare, I believe we should only move out as we receive confirmation from the Lord.

The Light of God and Revelation in the Night

After I explained my assignment, they felt the Lord would not have me come home for those 36 hours. So I made arrangements to stay with some close friends, who also happen to be intercessors. I went home and gathered some things, stopped at the store and bought my power bars and headed to the mountains again.

I reached the trail head at 4:45 p.m. and began to hike again. Now remember it is January and a bit cold. Not the greatest conditions for hiking, especially when it's going to get dark in a short time. I asked the Lord what He would have me to do first. He said, "All I want you to do tonight is to command the light of God on this spirit. Also, during this 36-hour period I do not want you to be praying for any individual people." So there I was, walking down hiking trails and forest service roads in the woods, loudly declaring the light of God to be on this spirit of Jezebel. I'm sure that the people that live down the hill wondered what a crazy man was doing yelling in the woods. During this time, as I would look at the spirit, it writhed in torment.

At about 8 p.m. a cold rain began to fall, so I put my raincoat on and headed back to my car. Soon after, I showed up at the door of my close friends. I was soaking wet and a bit worse for wear. They were gracious enough to let me spend the night in their spare room, as well as take a much needed hot bath. As I said goodnight, I told them that I would be leaving early the next day to head back into the woods. At this time, I did not tell them what my assignment was.

Prophetic Dreaming

In my dreams that night, the Lord gave me another piece of the puzzle about what I was dealing with. I had two dreams. The first was about a young man around the age of 18. We were on our way home from a youth outing and had stopped at a park to rest. All of a sudden, this young man was overcome with what I can only describe as murderous rage. He was screaming that he was going to kill this other young man that was there. Then the dream was abruptly over. Next I had a dream of another young man who was approximately 18 or 19. He was reading a text message from his phone that he had sent to another young man, asking if the other thought it would be okay to sleep with a boy while being high on drugs. As I awoke, I was very disturbed by both of these dreams. I instantly knew that this spirit of Jezebel was operating in conjunction with a spirit of anger and a spirit of homosexuality.

Back to the Woods

I knew I was on to something. I got up the next morning and headed right back to the same network of hiking trails and forest service roads that I was on the day before. As I began to hike, I asked the Lord about the strategy He had for the day. Once again He reminded me not to pray for any individual people during this time. He said He was going to show me the different ways that the spirit of Jezebel was operating in people's lives. He told me that as I would deal with the, what I call, "helper demons" that were assisting her, she would weaken. He also told me that before I could deal with these helper demons, I had to check my heart and repent personally for any way that I had agreed with them in my life. You can't deal with the enemy if he has a foothold in your life. Jesus said, *"Behold Satan comes and he has nothing in me."* (John 14:30)

As I hiked, it would take me roughly an hour to deal with each of these different demons. The reason is because the Lord also had me deal with the specific manifestation and operating mode of these spirits. So when I say that I dealt with, let's say, the spirit of anger, I didn't only deal with that spirit, but also confronted specifically how it worked in people's lives. During each hour the Lord would have me take time to praise, time to be joyful and time to shout victory. The Lord also instructed me that I was to declare the opposite of what these demons we're working in people's lives.

As I begin to explain to you about these different spirits, you may be tempted to think that one of these may apply to brother so-and-so or sister so-and-so. I would encourage you not to think about them, but let the Holy Spirit speak to you about where these spirits may have been attempting to operate in your life.

The first two I dealt with were a Jezebelic spirit of lying and a Jezebelic spirit of wounding. After I dealt with these spirits by taking authority over them and binding them, I looked again at Jezebel. She was still being held by the two angels and she was still very angry. But instead of standing erect she was hunched over. I knew she was getting weaker. I then sent a text message to my wife and our friend and said, "Jezebel is getting weaker." I received a text back that said, "We are here to hold up your arms as long as it takes."

I next dealt with a Jezebelic spirit of lust and a Jezebelic spirit of anger. Again this took about two hours as there were many different operating modes of these spirits. I looked at Jezebel again and this time she was even more hunched over, her hair was beginning to turn gray, and she was still very angry.

At this point I am about 7 to 8 miles out, so I decided to stop and take a rest. I brought along one of the power bars and had intended to eat it when the hike was over. As I sat down on the side of the road to look down upon a waterfall, the Lord said to me firmly, "You had better eat that power bar now." And was I glad that I did, because by this time I was beginning to get tired and my legs were very sore. After about a 20-minute rest, I started the journey back towards my car. It seems that the first four spirits the Lord had me deal with were preparation for the ones to come.

The next two that I dealt with were a Jezebelic spirit of homosexuality and a Jezebelic spirit of domestic violence. Many of the manifestations of the spirit of homosexuality were not necessarily sexually related. For example, one of the times that I asked the Lord, "Is there anything else about the spirit of homosexuality You want to show me?" He said, "Yes, in the infiltrating of friendships." Then I saw a vision of two men. One said to the other, "Boy my wife sure is a nag." "Yeah mine is too," the second replied. Then this spirit began to work to try to get those two men to value their relationship with each other more than their relationship with their wives.

Many times, as the Lord would show me specific manifestations of a spirit in the lives of Christian people, I would be very grieved. I would just groan and say, "Oh no, it couldn't be." And then I would deal authoritatively with that spirit and bind it. After I dealt with these two spirits I looked again at Jezebel. She was now even more hunched over, her hair was totally gray and her skin was beginning to turn a sick green color. As I looked at her face, she was still very angry at me. Then I noticed something else... she was completely blind. At this point I was beginning to get very tired and my legs were aching. I was not sure how much longer I would be able to continue.

Then the Lord showed me the last two spirits that I was to confront. They were a Jezebelic spirit of flattery and a Jezebelic spirit of control. These two spirits had the most individual manifestations. One that grieved me greatly was when I asked the Lord, "Is there anything else about this spirit of flattery You want to show me?" He said, "Yes, using flattery with the preaching anointing." This was very hard to hear. I groaned for a moment and then I spoke to this spirit as the anger of the Lord gripped me.

The spirit that had the most individual manifestations was the spirit of control. This is one of the most active spirits in the area of domestic violence. As I began to deal with this spirit, the Lord told me that when I finished battling it, the victory over Jezebel would be complete. I was very glad to hear that because I was quickly running out of steam. There were at least a dozen different ways that this spirit worked in the lives of people; such as control with intimidation, control by public ridicule of one's spouse, control by fear, and control by accusation and threats. Once I dealt with the final manifestation, I asked the Lord "Is there anything else about the spirit of control that You want to show me?" Then I heard Him say deep in my spirit. "No, you've got her."

I took one last look into the spirit realm and I could see these two detaining angels dragging Jezebel directly away from me and she was completely unconscious. Then one of the angels turned around and gave me a nod with a grin on his face as if to say, "Good job." I knew then that this spirit was completely defeated. My cell phone was just about dead, so I called my intercessor friend and asked her if she could pray and ask the Lord for confirmation that Jezebel was truly defeated. I turned my phone off to save the battery and turned it on a bit later to see that she had sent me a text message. The message read, "All I heard was, 'Now cleanse My people'."

At this point, it was within about 15 minutes of being 24 hours since I first began this assignment. Then the Lord spoke to me and said, "For the next 12 hours I am going to switch you back to a priestly ministry of intercession for my people." I had walked about another 2 miles to get back to the car, and then I drove to another friend's house to spend the night. On those two days I hiked approximately 27 miles. Not bad for a guy 50 years old who had been fasting for 30 days. But, of course, I know that it is the Lord who gives us strength to do what He calls us to do.

The Jezebelic Spirits

Here is a list of the spirits that I dealt with and the corresponding opposite truths that the Lord had me apply.

- Jezebelic Spirit of Lying Vs. Spirit of Truth (John 16:13)
- Jezebelic Spirit of Wounding Vs. The Power of Healing (1 Peter 2:24)
- Jezebelic Spirit of Lust Vs. Spirit of Purity (1 Timothy 5:22)
- Jezebelic Spirit of Anger Vs. God of Peace (Romans 16:20)
- Jezebelic Spirit of Homosexuality Vs. Male and Female (Genesis 1:27)
- Jezebelic Spirit of Domestic Violence Vs. Husbands Love Your Wives (Ephesians 5:25)
- Jezebelic Spirit of Flattery Vs. Knowing God, Doing Exploits (Daniel 11:32)
- Jezebelic Spirit of Control Vs. In Honor Preferring (Romans 12:10)

The Power of Seeing

Something I noticed during this time was that as I was able to see the spirits, somehow it released power and authority. The enemy primarily works in the darkness and as the Lord allows us to see things, they are brought into the light. The first time I saw Jezebel, I had this sense that she was angry at me primarily because I could see her. So I would speak to individual spirits, "I see you and I bind you in Jesus name." Somehow, in this seeing, they were brought to light which also brought victory.

"But solid food belongs to those who are of full age, that is, those who by reason of use have their senses exercised to discern both good and evil." (Hebrews 5:14)

The word "senses" in this verse is from the Greek word "Aistheterion" which means "organ of perception". As we spend time with the Lord, I believe our spiritual seeing and hearing will become clearer.

Understanding our Enemy
"Lest Satan should get an advantage of us: for we are not ignorant of his devices." (2 Corinthians 2:11)

I believe in these days the body of Christ needs to become keenly aware of two things. The first is, what is the Lord doing right now? And the second, what is the enemy doing? Many of us deal with negative issues based on the natural, earthly realm only. Not understanding that there is, quite possibly, a spiritual element. On the other hand though, I don't believe we need to go looking for demons to blame everything on. As humans we can mess things up quite well all on our own.

There are many times the enemy has been given entrance into our lives, and he must be exposed and defeated. We must also be careful in trying to assign the activity of certain demonic spirits to certain people.

I heard it said once that one of the earmarks of someone with the spirit of Jezebel is that they are continually accusing other people of having the spirit of Jezebel. We need to be very careful and ask the Lord for clarity and understanding, with confirmation. Then as the Lord gives the strategy we can move with confidence.

We have a God who is all about seeing the enemy defeated in our lives. So the Word says of Jesus that He was manifested to destroy the works of the devil. In Luke 4, we see Jesus going from defeating Satan in the wilderness, to proclaiming the kingdom in people's lives, setting them free from the ravages of the enemy. *"The spirit of the Lord is upon Me, because He has anointed Me to preach the gospel to the poor; He has sent Me to heal the brokenhearted, to proclaim liberty to the captives and recovery of sight to the blind, to set at liberty those who are oppressed, to proclaim the acceptable year of the Lord." (Luke 418-19)*

Today God is still working dramatically to defeat the enemy in people's lives. As followers of Jesus, part of our inheritance is to be those who are advancing the kingdom of God and beating back the kingdom of darkness.

The Spirit of Jezebel Today

The spirit of Jezebel is the primary spirit that is against people, ministries and churches, especially those who have a calling to the prophetic and intercession. There has been much destruction wreaked on the lives of many believers by this spirit. It has worked its way into churches, ministries, marriages, family relationships, and friendships.

The simplest way to describe a spirit of Jezebel is by the way it operates. Its very nature is control, manipulation and intimidation with a sexual element. It operates through people who sincerely believe they are being led and motivated by the Holy Spirit. It usually manifests through political maneuvering, selfish ambition, intimidating threats or seductive temptation. This spirit can work in men or women, leaders, young and old. It is very deceiving and very seductive. But we do not need to be fearful we just need to be aware.

The Spirit of Intimidation

Here is a great quote from John Bevere about intimidation:

"Countless Christians battle intimidation. Often those who are intimidated don't realize what they're fighting. As with most of Satan's devices, intimidation is camouflaged and subtle. We feel its effects—depression, confusion, lack of faith—without knowing its root. Had I realized I was intimidated, I would not have had such a struggle at that church. But I thank God for the lesson it taught me.

In frustration most of us deal with the aftermath, or fruit, of intimidation rather than intimidation in itself. Walk in your own God-given confidence and boldness." Walk in your own God-given authority, or someone else will take it from you and use it against you." (From the book Breaking Intimidation)

Often times the spirit of Jezebel works in unison with the spirit of intimidation. I had a dream that made this reality very clear. In the dream I was with some friends in a restaurant. The restaurant was owned by a woman, and her son was there. All of a sudden the son came up behind me and grabbed me by the back of the neck. He was pinching my neck very hard and I could not get free. My friends were paralyzed by fear. No matter how I tried, I could not get free. Finally, he let go, laughed at me and left.

The next scene was the next morning. I had come back with some other friends, those who would not be intimidated, to settle up with the son. The owner came out and told me that he was not there. I grabbed this woman by the neck and threw her up against the wall. With much authority in my voice I said this, "You tell him that if he ever does that to anyone again, I will come back here and put him in the hospital. Do you understand?" She said nothing, but just looked at me.

Then the son returned and came up from behind me, I grabbed him by the neck and threw him up against a wall. I said, "If you ever do that to anyone again, I will come back here and I will put you in the hospital. Do you understand?" His eyes were full of fear and he said," Yes I understand." That was the end of the dream. When I awoke, I instantly knew that the owner was Jezebel and the son was intimidation. In dealing with the spirits we must be forceful, fearless and authoritative. We must show no mercy and give no quarter. We need to take a stand in our personal lives as well as our churches and organizations.

The Jezebel Free Zone

I was having coffee once with a pastor who was having some trouble in his church. He asked me if I could come and spend some time prayer walking the facility. He said that in prayer he had seen a scroll and thought it had something to do with me. As I was praying at the church, God began to show me some things in a vision. Here is the letter that I sent the pastor about what I saw.

Hello Pastor,

Blessings to you brother. I went out Sunday morning and prayed about the possible assignment at your church. I heard the Lord say that I was to go and pray at the church grounds on Monday morning. So I went to the church at about 10 a.m. this morning, checked in at the office and told them that I had talked to you and that I would be walking around praying. They said that would be fine. I went into the sanctuary and sat down on the front row on the far right side. I asked the Lord about the scroll you had mentioned and He told me to open it and look at it. I looked in the spirit at the scroll and I saw written in the center the words, "JEZEBEL FREE ZONE." Then I saw on the four corners of the open scroll were written the words BLESSING, HONOR, GLORY, AND POWER.

BLESSING..HONOR

JEZEBEL
FREE
ZONE

GLORY...POWER

The Lord told me to walk around the building and the property and declare that this church is to be a "Jezebel Free Zone."

When I asked the Lord about the four words, this is what I heard Him say;

"This is a place that blesses Me."
"This is a place honors Me."
"This is a place that gives Me glory."
"This is a place that makes room for My power."

I walked around the sanctuary and prayed for the leadership and the worship team, that they would be free from the influence of the spirit of Jezebel, and that God would bless them. Then I went from the sanctuary and walked down to the intercession room. I prayed that the spirit of Jezebel would have no influence on the intercession that came from that place. Then I prayed a blessing upon the intercessors and I prayed for and blessed their leader.

After that, I went outside and prayed on the property and asked the Lord to arrest any Jezebelic spirit that was upon anyone the moment they drove into the parking lot. Then I prayed a blessing on the grounds and the property.

I believe the Lord has set angels on the property to arrest any Jezebelic spirit activity. However, I encourage you to have your intercessors pray further about the establishment of a Jezebel free zone. I will continue to pray and if I get anything else I will let you know. Blessings.

All for Jesus,
Mike

One of the purposes of intercession is to fill in the gaps around God's people so that the enemy does not get in. (Ezekiel 22:30) We need to declare every church, every ministry, every household a Jezebel free zone. If you are a pastor, leader or head of your home, you have authority to say no to the infiltration of the enemy and declare a boundary that will not be penetrated. Then in your own life there are things you can do to help fortify yourself against attack by this spirit. Determine to move in the opposite spirit at all times.

Often we take a lot of time rejecting and binding things away from us. Why don't we try binding something to ourselves? A good fortification against Jezebel is to make a declaration over your life on a regular basis. You can declare something like this, "I bind to my heart today purity, holiness, integrity and righteousness. You can declare that you yourself are a Jezebel free zone.

Quotes from Authors

Here is what some have said about the spirit of Jezebel:

"There is a war, a very ancient war, between the spirit of Elijah and the spirit of Jezebel. In this age-old battle, Elijah represents the interests of heaven: the call to repentance and the return to God. Jezebel, on the other hand, represents that unique principality whose purpose is to hinder and defeat the return of the church to God. To understand the conflict between the Elijah spirit and the spirit of Jezebel, we must understand these two adversaries as they are seen in the Scriptures. Each is the spiritual counterpart of the other. Is Elijah bold? Jezebel is brazen. Is Elijah ruthless toward evil? Jezebel is vicious toward righteousness. Does Elijah speak of the ways and words of God? Jezebel is full of systems of witchcraft and words of deceit. The war between Elijah and Jezebel continues today. The chief

warriors on either side are the prophets of both foes; to the victor goes the soul of our nation."
(Francis Frangipane from the article
"Elijah, Jehu, and the War against Jezebel")

"Jezebelic powers operating in conjunction with principalities and powers that torment people (Ephesians 6:12) these demonic powers include spirits of religion, manipulation, control, lust, perversion, and the occult. These spirits often work in concert with a Jezebel spirit to build strongholds in a person's mind. When a Jezebelic stronghold is established a person's mind, I define this as "coming under the influence of a Jezebelic spirit" at the moment this occurs the individuals rational reasoning process begins to deteriorate. His or her thoughts and actions become distorted."
(John Paul Jackson from the book
"Unmasking the spirit of Jezebel")

Final Thought and Prayer - As we move out in intercession and spiritual warfare, we must be aware of the tricks and traps of the enemy. Let's remain humble, teachable and dependent upon God. Let's allow the Holy Spirit to speak to us about any area where we are even taking one step towards agreeing with the spirit of Jezebel.

Father I thank you, in Jesus name, that the one reading this account about the spirit of Jezebel will walk free from any influence, any deception and any agreement with this spirit. I pray that you will use them mightily in the realms of intercession and they will be used by you to defeat this spirit in their own lives and the lives and many others. Amen!

Chapter 10
INTERCESSION AND WARFARE – PART II

A New Look at Spiritual Warfare

*"For the **weapons of our warfare** are not carnal, but mighty through God to the pulling down of strongholds"*
(2 Corinthians 10:4)

The Center Ground of Warfare

Spiritual warfare is one of those topics that is often misunderstood, and therefore sometimes avoided. On the other hand, it is often given too much attention. When I was a young believer I would hear of things like warfare, deliverance and demons and I would get this scary sick feeling that made me want to avoid such things.

I found that the more I understood, the less fearful I became, especially when it came to warfare. I discovered that it is so much more and so much less than what I first thought.

My first encounter with spiritual warfare came only a few months after I came to Jesus. I remember praying one night and this thought hit me, "I better be careful what I pray for or the devil will get angry and come after me." So I finished praying and went to sleep. Sometime in the night I had a dream that put things in perspective. In the dream I was in the corner of a dark room sitting on the floor. All of a sudden Jesus walked in and told me to trust Him and then left, shutting the door behind Him.

A few minutes later, the devil walked in and started to laugh and jeer at me. He came over and began to kick me as hard as he could. I wrapped my arms around my knees and buried my face for protection against his attack. Suddenly, in an instant of time, our positions were reversed and he was in the corner and I was kicking him!

I woke up with these thoughts: first, the devil will kick you when you're down and second, I didn't have to be afraid of the enemy anymore because Jesus was with me.

> *"And the God of peace will crush Satan under your feet*
> *shortly. The grace of our Lord Jesus Christ be with you. Amen."*
> (Romans 16:20)

In this chapter I want to take, what I call, the "center ground" on spiritual warfare; somewhere between a fearful avoidance of the matter and presumptuous overemphasis of it. I remember teaching on intercession and warfare at a conference in Madrid, Spain. Though the Spanish pastors wanted to embrace intercession, many of them wanted nothing to do with warfare. They thought that warfare was standing in the city square and rebuking the spirits over the city. They had heard horror stories of people who had tried such things with disastrous consequences. So they said, "If this is warfare, we don't want any of it." The problem was, they did not have a clear understanding of warfare; what it is and what it is not.

"Where there is no revelation, the people cast off restraint;
But happy is he who keeps the law." (Proverbs 29:18)

"If people can't see what God is doing, they stumble all over
themselves; but when they attend to what he reveals, they are most
blessed." (Proverbs 29:18 Message)

What I want to put forward is not an exhaustive teaching on warfare, but what I have learned in my journey as a warrior in the army of the Lord.

"No one engaged in warfare entangles himself with the affairs
of this life, that he may please him who enlisted him as a soldier.
" (2 Timothy 2:4)

The Greek word for soldier in this verse is *stratologeo*, which means: *to gather or select as a warrior, that is, enlist in the army, choose to be a soldier.* This is where we get the word "strategy" from. In warfare, we are not just randomly fighting, but carrying out the strategy of the Lord

Jesus the Ultimate Example

Jesus is the ultimate, most victorious warring king in the history of the universe. It would do us good to learn from His example and follow His leadership. Actually, dealing with the enemy was wrapped up in His whole purpose for coming to earth in the first place.

"For this purpose the Son of God was manifested, that He
might destroy the works of the devil." (1 John 3:8)

221

The word **manifested** is *phaneroo̅ and* it means *to render apparent - appear, manifestly declare, (make) manifest (forth)*. The word **destroy** is *luo* and if means *to "loosen" - break (up), destroy, dissolve, (un-) loose, melt, put off*. (Strong's)

> *"Behold, I give you the authority to trample on serpents and scorpions, and over all the power of the enemy, and nothing shall by any means hurt you."* (Luke 10:19)

In these verses, it appears to me that Jesus is planning to obliterate the works of the devil and his hordes and He wants to use us to do it. The key is to understand what our place and rank is in the army of the Lord, and how to operate in proper parameters. In earthly warfare, a soldier doesn't just run out and start shooting; there is protocol that has to be followed and there are lines of authority that must be considered. There are timing issues, strategy issues and maturity issues that must be addressed.

Defeating the Giants of Opposition

In March of 2007, my wife Darla and I went to Raleigh, North Carolina. We were able to attend a church to hear a great man of God named Frank Hultgren preach. Frank and June Hultgren are dear friends of ours from Perth, Australia. If you have been around me very much, you would have heard me refer to Frank (now in his 80s) as my mentor in intercession, warfare and the prophetic. The message that Frank brought was about Caleb demanding his promised inheritance at the age of 85. There is a spiritual principle we can learn about spiritual warfare from this Old Testament story.

*"And the LORD was with Judah; and **he drove out the inhabitants of the mountain;** but could not drive out the inhabitants of the valley, because they had chariots of iron. And they gave Hebron unto Caleb, as Moses said: **and he expelled thence the three sons of Anak.**"* (Judges 1:19 -20)

On the mountain of promise there is an enemy that does not want us to enter into our inheritance. We can learn some lessons from the enemies that Caleb and others in the Bible had to face. In warfare there are not only giants of opposition, but giants that want to steal, kill, and destroy.

Let's look at some of these giants, beginning with Anak and his sons:

- The name Anak means: *a necklace as if strangling chain, a collar.* This is a spirit that is trying to choke the life out people. This spirit is similar to the demonic spirit some refer to as a python spirit that strangles and smothers to steal the life away from a person.
- The next giant is Ahiman. His name mean: *brother of a portion (that is, gift).* This is the spirit trying to shut down the gifts of the Spirit from flowing in the Body of Christ. This would be the spirit of antichrist or "anti – anointing" spirit.
- The next giant is Sheshai. His name means: *bleached stuff, whiteness.* This is a religious spirit trying to turn colorful expression into pale religiosity. Have you ever had thoughts like, "Christianity sure is boring. The world seems a lot more exciting."? They are likely from this

spirit trying to get you in a place of colorless, mundane mediocrity instead a full life in the Spirit.

- The next giant on our list is Talmai. His name means: *to accumulate, that suspends the waters; heap of waters*. This is an opposing spirit trying to dam up the flow of spiritual power and provision. It attempts to put God's people under siege by cutting off the supply lines. This spirit especially attacks intercessors, givers and prophetic people. Suspending the waters is like the dropping of a slouch gate on an irrigation ditch. It won't take long for things to dry up and wither.

- In 2 Samuel 21:18, the giant Saph is mentioned. His name means *containment*. This is the spirit sent to bring containment on the Body of Christ. He is that which impedes and opposes growth on all levels. One of the things that Frank mentioned was a sign that he saw at Oral Roberts University (Frank was a professor there); the sign said "Make no small plans here." **Containment comes to keep our plans small, our faith weak, our success limited and our fruit shriveled.**

I think we need to rise up as Caleb did, kick these giants off our promised land and claim all of our Godly inheritance in Christ.

Winning Our Own Battles

One of the reasons a good number of Christians never enter the realms of intercession is because it is all they can do to win their own battles against the world, the flesh and the enemy's attacks. We all have personal struggles that we are dealing with in our lives, and if that is where you are, that's okay. But what we really need is believers who can not only win their own battles, but then go on to pray for and minister to others so that they can win great victories and advance as well.

When Israel was about to enter the Promised Land, there were 2 1/2 tribes that came to Moses asking if they could have their inheritance on the east side of the Jordan. He said they could, but first they would have to go into the Promised Land and fight for their brothers (Numbers 32). We need people who can effectively wage war in intercession on the behalf of others, but first we must learn how to win our own battles.

For many years I struggled with severe inferiority and rejection issues. This caused me to doubt God's ability and willingness to come through in my life, especially relating to my call to serve Him. I was bound by **"orphan"** thinking.

There was a time that I strongly believed God was calling me to take a team of intercessors to Scotland. The enemy began to challenge me on this when I was vulnerable. It was when I was away on a mission trip and the airplane flight had aggravated an abscessed tooth. I was in great pain because of the tooth; but at the same time, I was under an extremely heavy, demonic mental attack. The enemy was saying to me over and over, **"You are never going to Scotland! You will never pray there. You will never preach there. Never, never, never, never!"** I was under this mental attack for about three days. It was so bad that I was beginning to waver in my faith and believe the lie.

Just before a Sunday night meeting, I asked the mission team if they could pray for my tooth. I did not tell them about the mental attack. Suddenly, a sister on the team gasped and turned to me with a shocked look. She said, "I just heard the audible voice of God. He said, **'Tell him that all I have promised, I will do.'"**

That prophetic word completely defeated the mental attack I was under. It was as if that promise had then become a weapon for me to fight the enemy with.

About two weeks after returning home, the enemy came around with the same lie, but this time I had a different response. I said, "Oh really? Well I have a word from the Lord that says, all He has promised He will do." I took that word like a sword and cut the enemy's head off with it. Amazingly, he never tried to attack me in that way again. By the way, since then I have been to Scotland 11 times and lived there for three years. The enemy was wrong again.

Jesus used this same strategy in Matthew 4 to defeat Satan. He just declared the word of the Lord and won the victory. A verse that clearly describes this principle is 1Timothy 1:18 - *"This charge I commit to you, son Timothy, according to **the prophecies** (words from the Lord) previously made concerning you, that by them you may **wage the good warfare."** The Word of God is described as a sword in Ephesians 6:17, *"and the **sword** of the Spirit, which is the **Word of God**…"* The Greek word for "Word" is "rhema" which is commonly referred to as a present tense, personal word from God. The Word is also described as a sword in Hebrews 4:12, *"For the **word of God** is living and powerful, and sharper than* *any **two-edged sword**, piercing even to the division of soul and spirit, and of joints and marrow, and is a discerner of the thoughts and intents of the heart."* In the battle against our struggles and issues, isn't it great that God has given us such a powerful weapon to fight with? The Greek word for "Word" in this verse is *"logos"* which is referred to as the general, written Word of God. I believe we can take the prophetic words we have received plus specific Bible verses about our issue, as weapons to the battleground to fight with.

Whenever we are battling, if we take the Word and declared it over ourselves, the enemy will have no choice but to flee. It is not a selfish thing to speak the Word over ourselves. However, we must be focused and determined to declare the Word with authority.

For example, if you struggle with fear, you can take a verse like 2 Timothy 1:7 and pray it in this way: *"I declare in Jesus name that God has not given me a spirit of fear, but of power and of love and of a sound mind."* Or if you deal with depression you can pray Isaiah 35:10, something like this: *I declare in Jesus name that I will not be depressed because I have obtained joy and gladness, and sorrow and sighing shall flee away.* If inferiority, low self-esteem and an orphan mindset is your struggle, then in prayer declare a release of the spirit of adoption in your life. (Romans 8:15-17)

Some might say, "It is not that simple. I am dealing with serious issues that I have had for years." I don't see this as a quick fix but the beginning of a process. Much of our problem is that we have been reinforcing our issues with negative speech about ourselves. If we speak the Word instead, I believe we will see things change dramatically. Again, some might say, "Yeah, but what do I do if I stumble and fall back into my issue?" You get back up, ask for and receive forgiveness and start in again "speaking the truth" over yourself.

As you begin to overcome in areas of your own life, you will then be able to pray and declare God's victory over difficult issues in other people's lives. Remember, the definition of intercession is **focused prayer for others**. Whether it is praying for family, friends or others God would put on our heart, we can fight for them in prayer and see God do tremendous things in their lives.

The Protocol of Warfare

Understanding the protocol of warfare and its' many principals will help us effectively and safely extend God's kingdom on the earth. This applies to everything from praying off nightmares for your kids to onsite intercession in foreign countries.

It seems that in intercession and warfare, there are as many things not to do as there are to do. We must learn to know when to move forward in confidence and when to hold back from engaging the enemy.

The Principals of Warfare

I would like to share with you what I call the principals of warfare. These are the principles that I have learned and some stories of how I learned them. In the telling of the stories, I say things like, "The Lord said" or "The Lord showed me" or "I saw this or that". I am referring to my perception of what was happening in the realm of the spirit. Of course, I am a fallible human and "see in part" as Paul says. Therefore, my endeavor is to be as scriptural as possible so as to be on a solid footing.

*"But solid food belongs to those who are of full age, even those who because of use have their **senses exercised** to discern both good and evil."* (Hebrews 5:14)

Principal #1: We must allow God to work deep in us in order to allow the enemy no foot holds.

Graham Cooke put it this way, "You can't take ground from the devil if he has got ground in you." We are not talking about perfection here, but it is important to allow God open access to our hearts to let him deal with any issues that might be an obstacle as we enter into the realms of prayer. That is why character is so important.

Jesus said, "Behold Satan comes, but he has nothing in me." As the Holy Spirit does His job of conviction, every issue must be taken to the cross. Do you ever wonder why, many times when you go to pray, the first thing you end up doing is repenting for something the Holy Spirit is pointing out? The purpose is to clear the way for unhindered intercession.

One of the things we teach our intercessors before we take them to do onsite intercession is that they need to be ready for opposition in whatever area they are dealing with. Even though they may already be in the process of working on an area in their lives, we take them through a time of repentance to make sure that they have brought everything they are aware of before the

Lord. Then we remind them that they should not let their guard down even weeks after they get home. Any intercession is encroaching into enemy territory and the enemy will not be happy with you for it. Unfortunately, many Christians have adopted a "Don't bother me and I won't bother you" approach to the enemy. However, his goal is nothing less than absolute destruction in the lives of people. There can be no compromise. We will never grow out of our need for the Holy Spirit's voice to convict us of any area where we have agreed with the enemy - or our own carnal thinking for that matter.

Principal #2: In warfare you must always be led by the Holy Spirit.

> *"For as many as are **led by the Spirit** of God; they are the sons of God."* (Romans 8:14)

Warfare is not something you do on a whim or just because you feel like it. There must be an immediate reliance on the Holy Spirit as to what to do and how to go about things. It doesn't always have to be a long process. It does not take me long to hear the Holy Spirit when a member of my family is being attacked. Even then, there may be specific instructions He wants to give me. A good way to pray is, "Spirit of truth, will you show me what to do and how to pray in this situation?"

> *"And I will pray the Father, and he shall give you another Comforter, that he may abide with you forever; even the **Spirit of truth**."* (John 14:16, 17a)

This especially applies as you are interceding and you perceive evil entities in the spiritual realm. I remember once when my son and I went for a hike to the top of Spencer's Butte in Eugene, Oregon. When we got to the top I wasn't even thinking about spiritual things, but I soon became keenly aware of a strong demonic presence on the hilltop. They had become aware of my presence as well. I wasn't there to pray; I was there to spend time with my son. I said out loud, "I am not here to pray or confront anything so don't worry." We were then able to enjoy the rest of our time. We will talk more about properly engaging demon spirits later in this chapter.

Another instance was in 2005 when I had come to Edinburgh, Scotland. I was with a team to assist with two conferences on consecutive weekends in Manchester, England. I asked if we could drive up to Scotland between conferences so I could inquire of the Lord about taking a team of intercessors there. I climbed a hill in Edinburgh called Salisbury Crags while there. On the way up I heard the Lord say that there were six pagan spirits waiting for me at the top. Instantly, I knew by the Holy Spirit that I was not to confront these spirits at that time. As I approached the top, there were four Japanese tourists looking over the city. I said, "Lord, is this what you are talking about?" He said," No, just wait a few minutes." The Japanese tourists soon left and I went to the peak to see what I could see. I closed my eyes and instantly became aware of the six spirits. There were three on either side of me dressed in dark hooded robes. Edinburgh has one of the largest pagan festivals in the world called the Beltane Fire Festival. On April 30th each year, seven to ten thousand people gather to celebrate the "goddess of fertility" on another hill in the city. These were the demonic spirits working with the pagan leaders in the city. They said to me nervously, "This is our land." I responded with something that I instantly knew intuitively. I said "Actually, this is Gods land by creatorial right." I had never heard the word "creatorial" before, but it fit at the time. Then they said with a desperate tone, "Well the people are ours." I said "Well we will have to see about that won't we? And I am not talking to you anymore." Then I turned away and walked off the hill. Jesus never got into long conversations with evil spirits so neither should we.

Then there are times that we are aware of evil spirits, and He definitely wants us to act. I remember once, when I was praying at the church one morning, I saw something unusual in the spirit. I had been praying for my pastor's wife who had been plagued with severe migraine headaches for some time. As I prayed I saw a picture of her with a demon on her back. The unusual thing was that this demon had these long talons buried in her head. I said, "Lord what do you want me to do about this." He said, "I want three arrows in this demon now."

The Lord confirmed to me that this was Him, so I raise my spiritual bow. (I call it "spiritual mime" or acting out in the physical what you are doing in the spirit.) I shot three arrows in the direction of their house and felt a real release. This was about 7:30am. At about 8 o'clock the pastor came into the office. He said, "You won't believe it. This morning my wife was having tremendous pain from a migraine and then all of a sudden the pain was gone." I questioned, "Did that happen about 7:30?"

And he responded, "Yes exactly 7:30." I then told him the story. Praise God the spirit of infirmity was defeated.

Going On the Offensive

In our ministry, one of the exciting things we do is offer intercession support for outreach teams. One of the ways some of the Scotland ministries do outreach is by sending a team into a new age mind, body and soul fair. They set up a booth next to tarot card readers, new age practitioners, pagans and witches. They offer prayer for healing and spiritual readings (prophetic ministry). When they minister to people they tell them right up front that they are followers of Jesus. God has worked miraculously at these fairs through a couple of ministries called Glasgow Prophetic Centre and Light in Life.

I have been involved in several fairs with GPC in Glasgow, and also was part of the team at the largest psychic fair in the world in London in 2010. They have had many people saved and many instantly healed right there at the fair. My job at these outreaches was to provide the intercession cover for the team. I would stand 10 to 15 feet away and pray for the team and anyone receiving ministry. This allowed the team to minister without having to look over their shoulder. They previously had team members that had been actively cursed to their face by those at the fairs. My job was to see that did not happen. I am primarily there to protect the team. They started calling me Big Mike, which is from the movie Blindside. In the movie, Big Mike's job in football was to protect the team. Little did they know that Big Mike was my nickname growing up also.

There is one particular time at a psychic fair that I would like to tell you about. I was with Light & Life at a place called West Kilbride, Scotland. As the fair got going, I walked around the room and prayed quietly. I asked the Lord if there was anything He wanted me to be aware of. He replied, "Yes there is." I felt the hair on the back of neck stiffen. "Today we **go on the offensive**." Boy did He have my attention. He said, "I am really tired of this. I want you to walk around this room 12 times and **disallow illegal access into the spiritual realm**."

I believe the only right and legal way to enter the spiritual realm is through Jesus by the Holy Spirit. Jesus said, "I am the door." So I took about a half-hour to really pray about what the Lord was saying. I wanted to make sure that I was hearing properly. In warfare, there is no need for haste. Once I received confirmation from the Lord, I started to carry out the strategy by walking clockwise around the room. Those of the enemy's camp (witches, pagans and so forth) always march counterclockwise. I began to say under my breath, "I disallow illegal access into the spiritual realm in Jesus name." I said this over and over as I marched around the room.

What this meant for the practitioners was that they were no longer able to access information from demons, but had to bring something out of their soul to try to say anything meaningful to these people. When I was finished, I stood by a doorway. I asked the Lord to show me what was going in the spiritual realm. I saw a vision of an angel standing next to one of the tables where a man was reading tarot cards. The angel was standing there, as if on guard, with his arms folded. Next to him was a very angry demon. He was shouting at the angel saying, "He can't do this. We have a right to be here. He can't do this!" The angels did nothing but look at the demon and say, "Well he did it." and then remained on guard.

When I saw this, I burst into laughter. The enemy has legal rights until a son or daughter of God speaks, by the direction and authority of Christ, into a situation. The enemy then has to submit to that declaration. When we move out in warfare on assignment, we can have confidence that God is with us and will perform His word.

Principal #3: Do only what you are told to do. Don't add to the orders.
Part of being led by the Spirit is to not add to what He says. This was one of Adam and Eve's problems. The illustration from scripture is Jericho and Ai. In Jericho, Joshua was given explicit directions about how to win against a heavily fortified city. It probably seemed foolish, but it worked.

Sometimes in intercession and warfare we are called to do seemingly foolish things. I remember Graham Cooke saying one time, "As prophetic people we are called to unusual things at times, but in our life we should strive to be as normal as possible." I remember thinking at the time; "I think intercessors should have the same goal." I have been on a crusade for years to take the flakiness out of intercession. I think some see flakiness as a mandate rather than the exception. No wonder some pastors have a hard time wanting intercession in their churches. Now there is nothing wrong with manifestations and the like, but let's just make sure it's real. In Jericho Joshua prevailed, but in Ai it was another matter.

> *"They returned to Joshua and reported, 'Don't bother sending a lot of people--two or three thousand men are enough to defeat Ai. Don't wear out the whole army; there aren't that many people there.' So three thousand men went up--and then fled in defeat before the men of Ai!"* (Joshua 7:3-4)

In these verses, not only did they not add to God's orders, but they didn't even ask Him what the orders were. From then on it was common for the leaders of Israel to "inquire of the Lord" before a battle.

> *"And Jehoshaphat said unto the king of Israel, **Inquire**, I pray thee, at the word of the LORD today."* (2 Chronicles 18:4)

In any warfare situation we must ask, "Spirit of truth, what do you want us to do?" And then do only that.

In 1999 I went with an intercession team to Fez, Morocco to do covert onsite intercession. In the week before the trip we asked the Lord what we were to do in Morocco. He said two things. One was to physically bury the Word of God in the ground at the top of the city ramparts. The other was to read scripture out over the city.

While there we were visiting with some long time missionaries. They asked us about our plans at the ramparts and we told them what the Lord had shown us. They said that was great because a team came a few years earlier and went up there and started randomly rebuking spirits. Then after the team had left, the missionaries got beat up by the enemy for about six months. Lesson learned.

Principal # 4: In warfare, ask God for confirmation before you step out.

In the previous story, there was one part that I left out. The night before we left for Morocco, we gathered with some prophetic people to hear what the Lord might say about the trip. We had not shared our strategy with anyone. As we began to pray, a brother said he had a word for us. He said, "This is going to sound really strange, but I keep hearing the Lord say that you are to take Bibles and bury them in the ground over the city." We all began to laugh. Then as we told him that we had already bought the Bibles and that the Lord had already told us the same thing, he began to laugh as well.

> *"But the Lord is faithful, who shall **establish you** and guard you from the evil one."* (2 Thessalonians 3:3)

The Greek word for **establish** in this verse is *sterizo* which means *to confirm*. There are several reasons why we need confirmation before we step out in warfare. First off, there is the fact that God sees and knows so much more than we do. His wisdom, thoughts and ways are so much higher than ours. It would be wise for us to follow His lead and do it His way. Next is the confidence factor. It is very important not to move out in a stutter step fashion. When we have confirmation we can move forward with no hesitation. James 4:7 says, *"Therefore submit to God. Resist* *the devil and he will flee from you."* This is how that verse works. Submitting to God releases confirmation and then the enemy flees as we move forward in confidence.

Once I was leading a group of intercessors on a Tuesday night. The Lord had instructed me to break them up into groups of two or three to pray. After I gave them the instruction, I heard the Lord say to me that He wanted me to pray on the side alone. As I went over to the side of the sanctuary I was caught up in a vision. I was on an elevated rock in this field and all around me there were Christians with demons on their backs. I said, "Lord what do you want me to do?" He replied "I want you to take your rod and wave it over them." I said," Lord could you give me confirmation on that?" Almost before I finished asking the question the confirmation came with complete assurance.

One of the brothers in a small group across the sanctuary raised his voice and prayed loudly, "Lord as Moses lifted the rod in the wilderness we pray…" I had just received 100% go ahead and confirmation that I was seeing and hearing correctly. So I vigorously took my spiritual rod and began to wave it over the Christians in the vision. Then I began to weep in travail for what I was seeing. As soon as I began to wave the rod, these demons began to pop off like popcorn. It was a powerful time of warfare.

Shooting the arrows of the Lord's deliverance
*"And he said, Open the window eastward. And he opened it. Then Elisha said, Shoot. And he shot. And he said, the **arrow of the Lord's deliverance**, and the arrow of deliverance from*

Syria: for you shall smite the Syrians in Aphek, till you have consumed them." (2 Kings 13:17)

Another story of awesome confirmation happened on the trip to Ayutiya, Thailand that I previously mentioned. We had gone to several places to pray but one place seemed to draw our attention. We were staying at a hotel and I was rooming with a longtime friend of mine named Scott Sinclair. As we looked out our window we couldn't help but notice the (hundreds of feet high) Wat-Phrasisanphet Temple outside. One day I said to Scott, "I think the Lord is giving me a strategy as to how to pray at that temple. I think God wants us to deal with…" Then I was startled as he finished my sentence for me. He said "foundations." We knew we were on the right track. We asked the missionary if we could go there to pray. He said that would be good, but that he had never thought to take a team there before (our team was about the forth to come). It was strange, considering the fact that this was the highest structure for miles, dominating the sky line. As we prayed about going, the Lord gave us this verse, *"And he sent out **arrows**, and scattered them; lightning, and discomfited them. And the channels of the sea appeared; the **foundations** of the world were discovered, at the rebuking of the LORD, at the blast of the breath of his nostrils."* (2 Samuel 22:15-16)

The Lord told us that he wanted four arrows in each corner of the foundation of this 700-year-old temple. So then one afternoon, we all paid our entrance fee to get in, looking like American tourists. The team broke up to look around and Scott and I went about to fulfill our mission. We had checked with the team leader and he had released us to do the strategy. We went

239

to every corner of this temple that was surrounded by 20-foot statutes. At each corner I shot four spiritual arrows into the foundation of this evil place. As I was shooting, Scott stood in front of me just off to the left side. Later he told me that the Lord had given him a shield and that he was to protect me as I shot the arrows.

This sounds pretty strange, right? Well how did you think I felt playing spiritual Cowboys and Indians? If you think that is strange, wait until you hear what happened to us next. As we were finishing up, we had circumvented the temple and were coming back around to the main entrance. Then this thought went through my brain, "If we are really accomplishing anything, we should be getting some resistance from the enemy by now." A few seconds after I thought that, a woman came in the main entrance and aggressively started hissing at us like a vicious animal. I intuitively knew that we were not to face her, so we walked away. I then literally felt a demon jump on my back. I said "I don't think so, get off in Jesus name." The sensation left immediately. I soon glanced around and saw that the spirit had jumped back on her. She went from hissing to acting completely incoherent as if she was high on drugs.

We then gathered outside with the rest of the team the Lord showed us that there were going to be Buddhist who would come to that place to give their offerings and when they did, they would look up and would have an open vision of Jesus.

Principal #5: You must be clothed in the mantle of humility.

*"Likewise you younger people, submit yourselves to your elders. Yes, all of you be submissive to one another, and be **clothed with humility**, for God resists the proud, but gives grace to the humble."* (1 Peter 5:5)

As we enter the arena of warfare, if we approach with any pride in our heart, we are in danger. We must be clothed with the mantle of humility to not be open to attack. Pride is the very nature of Satan himself, and if we attempt to do warfare with the same motivation, he will have the advantage. I believe the mantle of humility is the undergarment for the armor of God. When we do onsite prayer with teams, I always have a time of actively putting on this mantle.

Principal #6: You must know the realms of authority

Staying in the place of your authority is crucial to warfare. Another attribute of Satan we want to avoid is rebellion. We need to make sure we are submitting to God's appointed authorities over us. In spiritual warfare there is no room for renegade lone rangers.

It is also important to understand the different areas of life that God has granted us breakthrough. Rees Howells called this, "The gained place of intercession" (A specific area of victory). You may be anointed to pray in one area and not so much in another. I have an anointing to pray for college students because it is one of the ongoing burdens that I carry. You may have another area that God has given you great grace and authority to pray into. This brings us to what I believe is the greatest "No No" in spiritual warfare.

Principal #7: We are NOT to confront and rebuke directly principalities and powers.

> *"The **heavens, even the heavens, are the LORD's**: but the **earth** hath he given to the **children of men.**"*
> (Psalms 115:16)

I do believe God wants to deal with these ruling spirits, but it will happen through a corporate anointing which releases the angels to fight. When they are in the air (second heaven) they are the Lords. When they touch earth, then we have all authority to bind and loose.

> *"Behold, I give unto you power to tread on serpents and scorpions,* **(earthly)** *and over all the power of the enemy: and nothing shall by any means hurt you."* (Luke 10:19)

This is how John Paul Jackson put it in his book, "Needless Casualties of War.": *"Accordingly, Carlos Annacondia of Argentina had a principality show up in his room. He had authority to rebuke the principality because it came into our terrestrial arena; the sphere Jesus empowered us to extend His kingdom, rule and reign. When principalities or other demonic beings in the second heaven invade our earthly realm, we have power to rebuke them. However, we don't have the anointing or the authority to wage war in the heavenly realms. We've only been commissioned to subdue the Earth."*

I knew a man that, as he was praying, saw a vision of the main principality over the city where he lived. In presumption, he assumed he was to take on this spirit by himself. So he stood toe to toe and rebuked the spirit. Over the next several years, I watched as this man went into, what appeared to be, strong pride and spiritual delusion. Later I asked God what happened to bring this on and He reminded me of the time this brother took on that spirit by himself. Please, let's be wise and not go there.

Someone might say, "Yeah, but how about those guys in South America who go into the city and confront principalities and powers and then God moves. What about them?" I would say, "Yeah, they're called Apostles." Most of us are not going be operating at that level.

The Daniel 10 Model

*"Then he said to me, 'Do not fear, Daniel, for from the first day that you set your heart to understand, and to humble yourself before your God, **your words were heard;** and I have come because of your words. But the **prince of the kingdom of Persia withstood me** twenty-one days; and **behold, Michael**, one of the chief princes, came to help me, for I had been left alone there with the kings of Persia. Now I have come to make you understand what will happen to your people in the latter days, for the vision refers to many days yet to come.'"* (Daniel 10:12-14)

Daniel interceded, which was his job, and the angels confronted the Prince of Persia (a principality). Our job is intercession and let God deal with and be concerned about the ruling spirits in the heavenly realms. Our intercession will enable those in the angelic realm to do war. Especially when praying for cities and regions, our part is to intercede.

What we are really talking about is called the *principal of displacement.* As we intercede, we bring the light into the darkness and darkness is displaced and pushed out.

Principal #8: Do not go to places of obvious evil without a clear word from the Lord.

This principle goes along with the previous one, in that we just can't go anywhere simply because we think it's a good idea. We must have confirmation to go and pray at a place of obvious evil. Many have acted foolishly in this area. I know of people who have gone to Masonic lodges, pagan festivals, places of false worship, places of sexual sin, and evil high places without a clear word, and have paid the price for it. Now there are times that the Lord will send us into these places to pray, but it is only as we have a clear word with confirmation. Also, we need to be submitted to local leadership, as well as have sufficient intercession cover for the prayer time. God is all about invading enemy territory, but it has to be done right and done carefully.

In 2007 I was planning to take a team to Scotland to go to five city centers and rededicate the people of Scotland to the Lord. The year before, I went with a team to visit a place in Edinburgh called Calton Hill. This is the site where the Beltane Fire Festival is held every April 30th. This is a pagan festival which celebrates the goddess of fertility. It is on par with Baal worship of the Old Testament. When we visited the site in the middle of the day on that Saturday afternoon in 2006, I was feeling nauseous the entire time I was there. I remember telling a team member that I thought this was one of the evil places I've ever been to. I said to myself, "I sure hope I never have to come back here again."

However, as we began making plans for the 2007 trip, one of my friends in Edinburgh sent an email and said, "By the way, you are going to be here during the Beltane Fire Festival. We have an outreach team going into the festival with a large group of intercessors staying behind to pray for the outreach. I immediately heard the Lord say, "Yes you are going into the festival". Later that day it was confirmed by a scripture about false worship in the Old Testament.

When we got to Edinburgh, we met with the outreach team and a group of 150 intercessors who were remaining behind to pray. As I and one other from our American team went into the festival with the outreach team, we encountered many people there just to watch. But there were also many very serious pagans who were engaging in heinous false worship. There was a procession around the grounds and then we were told that many would gather in a certain area to finish the night, which was the most evil part of the event.

We had a sense from the Lord that they were trying to release the demonic spirits into the atmosphere over Edinburgh. My friend and I were instructed by the Lord to pray that the demons would be contained on the hill and not go into the atmosphere. I knew intuitively that it meant these demons were going to go home with these people and torment them. Very sad for them in their deception.

Almost immediately after we prayed, the group that we were told would stay in that one spot got up all at once, moved about 200 feet away and started in again. So we moved over with them and prayed the same prayer again. After that, the group just broke up and they all went their separate ways.

The Beltane Fire Festival had been averaging about 10,000 to 12,000 a year in attendance. I was told in 2010 that the few years after the 2007 outreach team went in, the festival attendance had dropped dramatically each year. We believe God was doing something. I believe many of those same pagans are going to have a revelation of Jesus and come to the Lord.

Principal #9: Intimacy is the most crucial element of warfare
The most powerful lesson I have learned about warfare is the importance of just being in relationship and intimacy with Jesus. Then when He tells you to deal with the enemy, you do it with Him and have a terrific time doing it. The focus is always on Him and never only on what the enemy is doing. If we will stay in the center with Jesus, then we will destroy darkness and extend His kingdom in the earth. In these uncertain days we are living in, it is going to be very important to be "on the Lord's side". There is no other winning team in the universe.

*"Then Moses stood in the gate of the camp, and said, **who is on the LORD's side?** Let him come unto me. And all the sons of Levi gathered themselves together unto him."* (Exodus 32:26)

Final Thought - Not only is intimacy the most important factor in warfare, it is the foundation of intercession. This is the reason that it is the topic of the final chapter of this book. Join me as we look at our invitation to intimacy...

Chapter 11

AN INVITATION TO INTIMACY

Does He Really Love Me?

As individuals, the enemy attacks us most often in the area of our belief in God's love for us. We know it intellectually, and have read all the verses, but somehow the enemy still tries to talk us out of believing the fact that God loves us. It seems easy to believe that God loves other people, but when it comes to our personal lives there seems to be a nagging question mark. We find ourselves laboring under a performance mentality that is based on perfecting ourselves in order to be accepted. It starts when seeking acceptance by people, but somehow we end up thinking we need to do the same to find acceptance by God. I love what Philip Yancey said, *"There is nothing we can do to make God love us more, and there is nothing we can do to make God love us less."*

Many people, especially intercessors, struggle with what we call an *orphan mindset.* The orphan mindset is a pattern of thinking that often goes back to childhood. It has to do with thoughts, as well as emotions. If we continue in this mindset, it becomes a stronghold. This is a fortified citadel in our soul where the enemy dominates our thinking, emotions and self-perceptions.

The Oxford dictionary defines, "mind-set" as, "A habitual way of thinking," and "stronghold" *as, "A place that has been fortified against attack." "...casting down arguments and every high thing that exalts itself against the knowledge of God, bringing every thought into captivity to the obedience of Christ..."* (2 Corinthians 10:5)

I love this definition of a stronghold. *"A mind-set impregnated with hopelessness that causes us to accept as unchangeable situations that we know are contrary to the will of God."* (Ed Silvoso)

Some of the strongholds people deal with are: fear, resentment, bitterness, unforgiveness, apathy, unbelief, depression, anxiety, lust, anger, pride and greed. Many of these can open the door to addiction.

The orphan mindset (often referred to as the orphan spirit) can cause utter destruction in someone's life. The orphan mindset has brought more defeat, crippled more believers, ruined more relationships and derailed more destinies than just about anything the enemy can throw at an individual. It works with spirits of rejection, inferiority, fear, poverty and self-pity. It is one of the primary ways the enemy attempts to shut down intercession in someone's life. It is very difficult to stop and pray for someone else when you are battling this mindset.

"The orphan spirit is not something you can cast out because it is ungodly beliefs and/or attitudes of our flesh that has been developing over a lifetime. It has become part of our personality and character." (Jack Frost)

My Own Story of Victory

The orphan mindset is something I personally struggled with for many years. In my life it manifested primarily through inferiority and rejection. I've often said jokingly that, "I was going to write a book on rejection, but I was afraid nobody would read it." Now through a combination of powerful Sozo inner healing ministry and declaring the Word of God over my life, I am free from the chains of an orphan mindset. Sometimes the enemy tries to entangle my thinking and emotions in those chains again. However, what previously wrecked me for days or weeks, I now overcome in just a few minutes. It is so great to be free. Trust me, if I can walk free from this scourge, anyone can. Jesus said:

*"I will not leave **you orphans.***
I will come to you." (John 14:18)

The definition of the word *orphan* is, "A child whose parents are dead" (Oxford). Our heavenly father definitely isn't dead, and He loves us very much. Do you know that God loves you, yes you, so much that He comes into your room at night and stands by your bed, strokes your hair, sings songs over you and adores you? Zephaniah 3:17 says, *"The LORD your God in your midst, The Mighty One, will save; He will rejoice over you with gladness, He will quiet you with His love, **He will rejoice over you with singing.**"* Many of us could not imagine such a thing to be so, but it is.

I remember once I was standing by a lake on a dock just as the sun was going down. As I looked into the sky I beheld a breathtaking sunset. I don't know if you have figured this out yet, but God is the most amazing artist in the universe. I began to talk to the Lord, and I told him that I thought that the sunset was amazing. He said something to me that I did not expect. He said, "I'm glad you like the sunset because I made that one just for you." I said," But Lord, there has to be other people that are seeing the sunset. He said, "Yes, there is. But I made this one just for you." I was so overwhelmed with His love for me at that moment that I began to weep. It is a profound thought that the God of the universe would make an incredible sunset just for one of His.

Fruits of an Orphans Mindset

If we do not allow the Lord to bring us into freedom, the orphan mindset could bring some very harmful, rotten fruit into our lives. This way of thinking often opens the door to the fruit of having a poverty mentality. Because we think we're undeserving, we never ask for anything for ourselves. When many of us grew up, we were trained not to ask for things. We would go spend the night at our friend's house and we were told; "Now I don't go asking for a bunch of stuff." Rightly so, in case we got the idea to start rifling through our friend's refrigerator. But in God's house, He wants you to feel right at home. He wants you to be so familiar with Him that you're not afraid to ask him for something. How many times did Jesus tell us to ask? Many of us have an attitude like Oliver Twist. We go to God and say, "Please sir, can I have some more?" Scripture is clear that God loves us very much and wants us to have the freedom to ask Him to meet our needs.

Another fruit born out of the orphan mindset are vows of self-protection. It often becomes a defense mechanism to prevent further wounding. It causes us to look at people with suspicion, especially people who remind us of those who previously hurt us. The vows we make usually start with the words, "I'll never...." These kinds of statements give the enemy legal right to keep binding us up.

The next fruit is that we end up living with this continual feeling of being in trouble. We live with a knot in our stomach for no apparent logical reason. We just feel like we're not getting "it" right, even if we don't know what "it" is. It is that feeling you get when you have done something wrong and you know you're about to get severely corrected by an unloving authority such as a mean parent, boss or teacher. The problem is that you're not in trouble, but you feel in trouble.

I have actually had times when I was going through my day and noticed that I had this anxious feeling in my stomach. I would then think really hard about what might be wrong. Then I would ask the Lord if He knew of anything. After that if I could not put my finger on it, I knew that it was from the enemy. I would then declare, "Whatever this is, I command you to leave now in Jesus' name" and the feeling left. It is not our inheritance to go around with this sick feeling or overwhelming thought that I'm getting it wrong and I'm in trouble. Orphan thinking is all about performance and how I am not measuring up in someone's eyes. God wants you to know that He loves you, is for you, and you are not in trouble. He will bring conviction, but never condemnation.

The next rotten fruit is twisted perceptions. When we're dealing was something like rejection, it affects us deep in our emotions. Now there's nothing wrong with emotions. Where it goes wrong is when the enemy brings a lie into our mind and we filter it through our emotions to make it seem more real. We have come to believe that if our emotions tell us something, it has to be real. I'm here to tell you that it isn't. Just because a thought goes through our emotions and we have an emotional response, it does not change the fact that what was communicated is still a lie. It goes through our orphan mindset filter and because we feel it, we are tempted to believe it.

This especially applies to entire areas of rejection. People will reject us for various reasons. The only problem is that when we have an orphan mindset, rejection on the level of a 3 or 4 is perceived as a 9 or 10. Our reaction to the rejection and our personal offence relating to it are much worse.

We can react to a perceived rejection that is not even real. How many of us, when someone has given us a strange look, we just knew they had something against us? When we got the courage to go and see what was wrong, they told us everything was fine, and there was nothing there. We got all wrecked inside for nothing. We need to let the Lord heal us from an orphan spirit; then we will be able to have proper perceptions of what is really going on, and go on to forgive those who reject us.

There are many other negative fruits that come from an orphan mindset; things such as the sense of feeling left out, the temptation to isolate and withdraw, loneliness, depression, suspicion and mistrust, just to name a few. We must come into healing and realize that Jesus took all this for us so that we don't have to carry it ourselves.

"He is despised and rejected by men, A Man of sorrows and acquainted with grief. And we hid, as it were, our faces from Him; He was despised, and we did not esteem Him. Surely He has borne our griefs And carried our sorrows; Yet we esteemed Him stricken, Smitten by God, and afflicted." (Isaiah 53:3-4)

Spirit of Adoption

The answer to an orphan spirit is the spirit of adoption. *"For ye have not received the spirit of bondage again to fear; but ye have received the Spirit of adoption, whereby we cry, Abba, Father."* (Romans 8:15)

My wife Darla and I had the privilege of adopting three of our five children. I thought it very interesting that when we went to the lawyer's office to finalize the adoption, we were presented with a new birth certificate for the child. This birth certificate legally rewrote their history. The word adoption is nowhere on the certificate. It states their new name and that they were born into our household on their birthday. When we are born again into God's family, we are not seen as wanna-be children, but actual children. God wants us to be baptized in the spirit of adoption and confront every thought, every emotion, and every word that is not in agreement with His love for us.

The Invitation to Intimacy

Once we begin to gain victory over an orphan mindset, we will discover that there is a heavenly invitation being offered to us. It is the divine invitation to intimacy. The actual invitation transcends what we can even begin to imagine of God's heart towards us. His desire is to know us and have us know Him.

We are invited to go beyond surface-level acquaintance into intimacy.

You might say to yourself, "What does intimacy have to do with intercession?" The answer is **everything.** Of all the things we have discussed in this book about intercession, **intimacy with the Lord is the most important of all of them.** It is to be the basis and foundation of all prayer and intercession. If intimacy is not that which leads us into, carries us through and brings us to a place of breakthrough, we are missing the mark. Let's look at this amazing invitation that we are being offered.

The reality of intimacy is rooted in the phrase, "To know." The Hebrew word for "know" is yâda. This is an interesting word. It is the word used to describe physical intimacy between a man and wife in the book of Genesis. We often think of the marriage relationship as being the closest possible of all relationships. God wants to communicate that His desire for our relationship with Him is even deeper and closer than a marriage relationship.

> *"Teach me your ways so that I may know you and*
> *continue in your favor."* (Isaiah 43:10)

It is also interesting that the first mention of the word yâda is used to describe the moment when Adam and Eve knew they were naked. In that moment they knew that the intimacy of their relationship with God was replaced by shame. God even uses the word "know" in Proverbs 3:5-6. I especially like how the Young's Literal Translation puts these verses, *"Trust unto Jehovah with all thy heart, And unto thine own understanding lean not. In all*

thy ways know thou Him, *And He doth make straight thy paths."* (YLT)

The connotation is that we should know Him intimately in every area of life. God doesn't want to be just a slice on the pie chart of your life. He wants to be in and through, over and under, and surrounding you. He wants to be your first love as you pursue Him with all of your heart, soul, mind and strength. This is why the first commandment is called the first commandment. There's nothing more important than your loving relationship with God. Everything we do and everything we are for the duration of time is to spring forth from the intimacy of relationship with Him. This is the immeasurable love that God wants us to be rooted and grounded in. (Ephesians 3:17-19) The Greek word for *"know"* is *"Ginōsko"* which is *"to know"* *(absolutely). "This is Eternal Life: that they may know you, the only true God, and Jesus Christ, whom you have sent."* (John 17:3)

> *"Not everyone who says to Me, 'Lord, Lord,' shall enter the kingdom of heaven, but he who does the will of My Father in heaven. Many will say to Me in that day, 'Lord, Lord, have we not prophesied in Your name, cast out demons in Your name, and done many wonders in Your name?' And then I will declare to them, '**I never knew you**; depart from Me, you who practice lawlessness!' "* (Matthew 7:21-23)

Intimacy with the Three

"I bind unto myself the Name, the strong Name of the Trinity, by invocation of the same, the Three in One, and One in Three, of Whom all nature hath creation; Eternal Father, Spirit, Word: praise to the

Lord of my salvation, salvation is of Christ the Lord. Amen." (From St. Patrick's Breastplate Prayer)

The invitation becomes more personal when we realize we are called to have relationship with each member of the Trinity. It is a deep fellowship with each member of the Godhead that we are invited into.

The sacrifice of Jesus opened the way for us to enter into a love relationship with the Father, the Son, and the Holy Spirit. This relationship is described in John14:19-26:

> *"'A little while longer and the world will see me no more, but you will see me. Because I live, you will live also. At that day you will know that I am in **my Father** and **you in me**, and **I in you**. He who has my commandments and keeps them, it is he who loves me. And he **who loves me** will be **loved by my father**, and **I will love him** and manifest myself to him.' then Judas (not Iscariot) said to him, 'Lord, how is it that you will manifest yourself to us, and not to the world?' "*

The Father - Greatest Dad in the World

Our Heavenly Father is the perfect father in every way. Jesus came to reveal the Father to us. God was never referred to as Father until Jesus came. It is no accident that the first words used in the Lord's Prayer are, "Our Father." It was like he was saying, let me introduce you to our wonderful Father who so wants to have relationship with you. I believe Jesus is drawing from His own relationship with the Father from eternity past in communicating who the Father is to us. Jesus' call to have us become like little children is so we can connect with Father God.

I love the imagery of me, as a child, sitting on Daddy's lap. There is no place more loving and safe in all human existence.

If we have what is commonly referred to as "father issues," we need to come into healing in these areas so that our relationship with Father God can be unhindered. Let's determine not to let our tarnished images of what a father is stop us from this relationship.

> "Behold what manner of love the Father has bestowed on us, that we should be called children of God! Therefore, the world does not know us, because it did not know Him." (1 John 3:1)

> "What marvelous love the Father has extended to us! Just look at it—we're called children of God! That's who we really are. But that's also why the world doesn't recognize us or take us seriously, because it has no idea who he is or what he's up to." (1 John 3:1 Message)

Jesus – Wonderful Savior, Greatest of Friends
> "That which we have seen and heard we declare to you, that you also may have fellowship with us; and truly our fellowship is with the Father and with His Son Jesus Christ." (1 John 1:3)

> "No longer do I call you servants, for a servant does not know what his master is doing; but **I have called you friends,** for all things that I heard from My Father I have made known to you" (John 15:15)

Since Jesus was the one who brought us salvation by His death on the cross, He is the member of the Trinity that most of us were first introduced to. Just the fact that He saved me from an eternity in hell makes me want to love Him. But he is so much more than that. He is the multi-faceted Savior in whom we will have eternity to fully discover. In the scripture there are over 100 different names and titles for this One we love. He is our savior, our captain, our king.

One of the ways we get to know Him is by the great privilege of immersing ourselves in the gospels. I remember someone saying that knowing about God is not the same as knowing Him. I agree with that to an extent. Knowing about him by reading the scriptures about His life, and hearing the things He said, is a great place to start getting to know Him.

"One thing I have desired of the Lord, that will I seek: that I may dwell in the house of the Lord all the days of my life, to behold the beauty of the Lord, and to inquire in His temple." (Psalms 27:4)

Holy Spirit - The Helper Who Comes To Fill and Live Within

"Now hope does not disappoint, because the love of God has been poured out in our hearts by the Holy Spirit who was given to us." (Romans 5:5)

God wants to be so close and intimate with us that He sent the Spirit, not to just come upon us, but to live within us.

"But you are not in the flesh but in the Spirit, if indeed the Spirit of God dwells in you. Now if anyone does not have the Spirit of Christ, he is not His." (Romans 8:9)

Developing sensitivity to the Holy Spirit is very important. So often the soul becomes noisy and distracted. It is then that the still small voice of the Holy Spirit becomes difficult to tune into. We need to allow ourselves to become still and step away from distraction. We need to live every day with the revelation that He is right here with us. He is only a whisper away.

One of the things I've learned to do in my relationship with the Holy Spirit is to be quick to ask questions. We have at our disposal the wisdom and knowledge of the ages. The ancient library at Alexandria has got nothing on Him. All the vast knowledge acquired in universities around the world is a drop in the bucket compared to His vast knowledge, insight, and wisdom.

I often find myself trying to figure things out on my own and struggling to find my way. All along the Holy Spirit is right there to talk to me, encourage me, give me instruction and share His wisdom with me. Reliance and dependency on the Holy Spirit must be given priority. We must develop a deep love relationship with the Holy Spirit. Speak directly to Him and tell him that you love Him, worship Him, and adore Him. Thank Him for all that He does and for who He is to you.

Ways of Intimacy

When I was a young believer, I used to hear messages on how I should be as a Christian. But often the message came with no practical wisdom on how to walk that out. Even by reading this book, you have already entered into intimacy with the Lord to a certain extent. God desires to take you to the next level. Let's look at some practical ways to answer the invitation to come into intimacy with God.

- **Know Him In His Goodness.**

    "Oh, give thanks to the LORD, for He is good! For
    His mercy endures forever." (Psalms 136:1)

We must know Him in his goodness because if we do not believe wholeheartedly that He is good, we will not want to pursue knowing Him. We must believe that he is100% good, 100% of the time. Our adherence to the goodness of God is often tested in the midst of contradictions of faith. No matter what difficulty or heartache, setback or devastation, grief or disappointment, we must never allow ourselves to be, even slightly, removed from the foundation of God's goodness in our life.

It is this revelation of goodness that allowed Paul and Silas to be singing praises in prison. It is this revelation that allowed martyrs to be singing and rejoicing in the midst of their lives being taken. It is this revelation that will allow us to endure to the end, knowing Him who is from the beginning.

- **Knowing Him in Worship**

God is looking for people who will be abandoned worshipers. The problem is the paradigm that many people have made the word "worship." Worship is not just a time during the Sunday morning meeting to get us in the right frame of mind to hear good preaching. It can do that, but worship is of tremendous value and stands alone as such. Worship is an end all to itself.

Worship is at the heart of why we were created. Do you know it is our destiny and purpose to know Him and worship Him? You were created to love him for eternity. You were created to stand in his presence and love Him and adore him. Whether it is corporate worship or worship during our individual devotion time, we must know the Lord as we behold him in worship. Let's ask God to give us a heart to be a passionate pursuer of Him in worship.

- **Knowing Him in Daily Prayer**

"My voice you shall hear in the morning, o Lord; in the morning I will direct it to You, and I will look up. (Psalms 5:3)

Of course, much has already been said about prayer. But let's look at prayer as a means to knowing Him. Every day prayer is one of the main ways that we are continually brought back into relationship with Jesus. It keeps us in a place of *praying without ceasing* which is simply communing with the Lord throughout the day.

This is what Matthew Henry's Commentary said about praying without ceasing:

"The way to rejoice evermore is to pray without ceasing. We should rejoice more if we prayed more. We should keep up stated times for prayer, and continue instant in prayer. We should pray always, and not faint: pray without weariness, and continue in prayer, till we come to that world where prayer shall be swallowed up in praise. The meaning is not that men should do nothing but pray, but that nothing else we do should hinder prayer in its proper season. Prayer will help forward and not hinder all other lawful business, and every good work."

We must realize that prayer is one of the greatest things we can involve ourselves in. We have an invitation from the king of the universe to spend time with Him and get to know Him every day. The One who is spinning galaxies on His finger wants to have time with you. He wants you to get over the feelings of unworthiness and come into His presence and be with Him. He has made a place for you at his table. You have been invited to come into a place where you can talk about anything with Him.

Here are some great prayer quotes:
"Is prayer your steering wheel or your spare tire?"
(Corrie Ten Boom)

"Those who know God the best are the richest and most powerful in prayer. Little acquaintance with God, and strangeness and coldness to him, make prayer a rare and feeble thing." (E. M. Bounds)

"Pray, and let God worry." (Martin Luther)

"Prayer is not so much an act as it is an attitude—
an attitude of dependency, dependency upon God."
(Arthur W. Pink)

"When a Christian shuns fellowship with other Christians, the devil
smiles. When he stops studying the bible, the devil laughs. When he
stops praying, the devil shouts for joy." (Corrie Ten Boom)

"Prayer does not fit us for the greater work, prayer is
the greater work." (Oswald Chambers)

- **Know Him in the Word**

Much of the conversation that you will be having with the Lord in prayer time will be around His Word. As the Holy Spirit unlocks the scriptures about Jesus, what He reveals will cause us to fall more deeply in love with Him (John 14:26). Of course, Jesus Himself is referred to as the Word. As we begin to know the Bible, we will know how He thinks, how He feels, and how He is. This is why meditating on scripture is so important. We need to saturate ourselves in, not just the whole Bible, but a few verses at a time, to be impacted by the depth of meaning as it goes from our head to our heart. Then truly the spirit of wisdom and revelation in the knowledge of Him will be ours.

"This Book of the Law shall not depart from your mouth,
but you shall meditate in it day and night, that you may observe
to do according to all that is written in it. For then you will make
your way prosperous, and then you will have good success."
(Joshua 1:8)

Intimacy Quotes

Here are some great quotes on the subject of intimacy with the Lord:

"We are at this moment as close to God as we really choose to be. True, there are times when we would like to know a deeper intimacy, but when it comes to the point, we are not prepared to pay the price involved." (J. Oswald Saunders)

"Those who know God the best are the richest and most powerful in prayer. Little acquaintance with God, and strangeness and coldness to Him, make prayer a rare and feeble thing." (E. M. Bounds)

"To fall in love with God is the greatest of all romances; To seek Him, the greatest adventure; To find him, the greatest human achievement." (Augustine)

"A man who is intimate with God will never be intimidated by men." (Leonard Ravenhill)

"The best cure for loneliness is developing an intimate relationship with Jesus Christ." (Anonymous)

The Vision of the Gates - Riding With Jesus

I would like to share with you one last story that illustrates what I believe God is really wanting to communicate relating to intimacy with Him.

Several years ago I was on the front row, during the Sunday morning meeting at our church in North Carolina. We had a guest speaker that morning. As he began to speak, I noticed something unusual on the floor next to the pulpit. He had a bottle of white wine and two wine glasses. I later found out that it was water instead of white wine. Towards the end of his message he picked up one of the glasses and the bottle and told us that he had a prophetic word for the church. He began to fill the wine glass as he said, "The Lord says that He is going to come, and He is going to keep coming and He is going to keep coming and He is going to keep coming… He kept pouring and the water began to overflow all over the front of the stage. At that moment a powerful wave of the Holy Spirit flowed over the congregation.

I was instantly swept into a vision that was life-changing. In the vision, I saw Jesus come up to me on the front row and start taking off my armor and setting it aside. Then He grabbed me by the hand and took me back through my life. We would stop at certain hurtful times in my life and the Lord would intervene in the situation. We went all the way back to where I was four or five years old, then we started back. When we arrived back on the front row, the Lord put back on my armor and said, "Come with me." Waiting were two horses that we quickly mounted, and we were off. I looked over at the Lord and noticed that He was in full battle array and that he had a huge smile on his face. I could not believe that this was actually happening. I was right even with Jesus. The excitement was incredible.

We rode and laughed without a care until we came to these two massive gates, hundreds of feet high. He said, "Stop" so we dismounted and walked up to the gates. I noticed that each gate had a giant handle made of metal. Jesus said, "Grab that handle right there." I instantly thought to myself, "I can't open this gate." But then I reasoned that if Jesus was the one asking, I might as well give it a go. As He pulled on the left and me on the right, the gates swung wide open. Then to my surprise, I watched as tens of thousands of captives stormed through the gates shouting for joy at their newfound freedom. The enemy was being defeated and the captives were being set free.

After the last captives had passed through the gates, Jesus said, "Let's go." We mounted the horses and began to ride again. We were laughing and crying, overwhelmed by the joy of being together. Then He said, "Wait. Stop." I thought maybe we were going to do some more warfare or maybe there were more captives to be set free. But no. We climbed off the horses and He grabbed me up in this huge hug that seemed to last for at least five minutes. He kept saying over and over, "Isn't it just great to be together? Isn't it just great to be together? The end of the vision had Jesus and me hugging and crying, just so happy to be together. This was friendship at a level that I could only imagine.

You see, intercession and warfare is mostly about just being with Him. It's about being enveloped in the truth and actuality of His words to us, **"Isn't is just great to be together?"** Then, in the mist of loving Him, we take a little time, pray for release and breakthrough, defeat the enemy and set the captives free.

As believers, intimacy with God not only is a tremendous privilege, it is our inheritance. To know, love and glorify Him who is from the beginning will be our greatest joy for eternity.

The invitation to intimacy is for us now, and it is to become a foundation for the rest of our lives.

Final Thoughts - My hope is that the thoughts and stories in this book have been an encouragement and inspiration to you. My prayer is that God will use you mightily in intercessory prayer and you will find a life of adventure, fulfillment and fruitfulness in Him.

"Now to Him who is able to do exceedingly abundantly above all that we ask or think, according to the power that works in us, to Him be glory in the church by Christ Jesus to all generations, forever and ever. Amen." (Ephesians 3:21-22)

BIBLIOGRAPHY

Chapter 1

Norman Grubb *Rees Howells Intercessor* CLC Publications (January 1,1988)

Dutch Sheets *Intercessory Prayer* Bethany House Publishers (March 3, 2008)

Beni Johnson *The Happy Intercessor* Destiny Image (February 1, 2009)

Oswald Chambers *My Utmost for His Highest* Discovery House; Revised edition (August 1, 2012)

David Yonggi Cho *Prayer: Key to Revival* W Pub Group (October 1984)

Chapter 3

Ed Silvoso *That None Should Perish: How to Reach Entire Cities for Christ Through Prayer Evangelism* Chosen Books (April 18, 1995)

Chapter 8

John Dawson *Healing America's Wounds* Regal Books (February 1997)

Chapter 9

John Bevere *Breaking Intimidation* Charisma House; Revised edition (December 6, 2005)

John Paul Jackson Unmasking the spirit of Jezebel Streams Pubns; Reissue edition (January 1, 2002)

Chapter 10

John Paul Jackson Needless Casualties of War Streams Pubns; 6/15/99 edition (July 1, 1999)

Chapter 11

Philip Yancey *What's So Amazing About Grace?* Zondervan; Revised ed. edition (February 1, 2002)

Ed Silvoso That None Should Perish: How to Reach Entire Cities for Christ Through Prayer Evangelism Chosen Books (April 18, 1995)